FAMILY WALKS AROUND DUBLIN
A WALKING GUIDE

ADRIAN HENDROFF is a member of the Outdoor Writers and Photographers Guild, Mountain Training Association and Mountaineering Ireland. His articles and photographs have featured in *The Irish Times, Irish Examiner* and magazines such as *Trail, Outsider, Mountain World Ireland, Walking World Ireland, TGO, Irish Mountain Log, Trek & Mountain* and *Walking Wales Magazine*. For more information, visit Adrian's website and online gallery at www.adrianhendroff.com

You can also keep up to date at:

facebook.com/adrianhendroff.exploreirelandsmountains
twitter.com/exp_ireland_mtn

Also by Adrian Hendroff

The Beara and Sheep's Head Peninsulas: A Walking Guide
The Dingle, Iveragh & Beara Peninsulas: A Walking Guide
The Dingle Peninsula: A Walking Guide
Donegal, Sligo & Leitrim: Mountain & Coastal Hillwalks
From High Places: A Journey Through Ireland's Great Mountains
Killarney to Valentia Island, The Iveragh Peninsula: A Walking Guide

The view towards Kelly's Glen from the western slopes of Fairy Castle.

Disclaimer

Walking and hillwalking are risk sports. The author and The Collins Press accept no responsibility for any injury, loss or inconvenience sustained by anyone using this guidebook.

To reduce the chance of break-in to parked cars, walkers are advised to place all valuables and belongings out of sight.

Advice to Readers

Every effort is made by our authors to ensure the accuracy of our guidebooks. However, changes can occur after a book has been printed, including changes to rights of way. If you notice discrepancies between this guidebook and the facts on the ground, please let us know, either by email to enquiries@collinspress.ie or by post to The Collins Press, West Link Park, Doughcloyne, Wilton, Cork, T12 N5EF, Ireland.

Acknowledgements

There are several people whose encouragement, participation and support were invaluable during the making of this guidebook, and to whom I owe a huge debt of gratitude. In particular, I would like to thank my wife, Una, for the proof-reading, love and support. Thanks also to The Collins Press for the continued support in my work, and for your expertise as always. And finally thanks to Sarah, Niamh, Ciara, Emma, James, Aaron, Thomas, Joe Junior, Stephen, John O., John N., Sinead, Una, Kay, Shirley, Greta, Jeanne, Caitriona and Tanya who have accompanied me on some of the walks. Also in special remembrance of my late grandfather John Hendroff who passed away peacefully during the writing of this guidebook.

FAMILY WALKS AROUND DUBLIN
A WALKING GUIDE

ADRIAN HENDROFF

The Collins Press

For all the family, with love

First published in 2017 by
The Collins Press
West Link Park
Doughcloyne
Wilton
Cork
T12 N5EF
Ireland

A CIP record for this book is available from the British Library.

Paperback ISBN: 978-1-84889-311-5
PDF eBook ISBN: 978-1-84889-632-1
EPUB eBook ISBN: 978-1-84889-633-8
Kindle ISBN: 978-1-84889-634-5

Design and typesetting by Fairways Design

Typeset in Myriad Pro

Printed in Poland by Białostockie Zakłady Graficzne SA

Contents

Route Location Map

Route 1: Ardgillan Castle, Park and Demesne

Route 2: Skerries *Slí na Sláinte*

Route 3: Donabate Coastal Walks

Route 4: Malahide Marina, Estuary and Castle

Route 5: Portmarnock to Malahide Coastal Walk

Route 6: Ireland's Eye

Route 7: Howth Northern and Eastern Loop

Route 8: Howth Southern Loop

Route 9: St Anne's Park

Route 10: North Bull Island Loop

Route 11: Irishtown Nature Park and Poolbeg Lighthouse

Route 12: Phoenix Park

Route 13: Grand Canal and Dublin City Loop

Route 14: Dodder River Walk and Bushy Park

Route 15: Marlay Park

Route 16: Sandycove Heritage Trail

Route 17: Dalkey Quarry and Killiney Hill Circuit

Route 18: Rathmichael Woods Circuit

Route 19: Lead Mines Chimney and Carrickgollogan

Route 20: Barnaslingan Trail and The Scalp

Route 21: Prince William's Seat and Raven's Rock from Glencullen

Route 22: Three Rock Wood and Three Rock Mountain from Ticknock Lower

Route 23: Fairy Castle, Two Rock Mountain and Three Rock Mountain from Ticknock Upper

Route 24: Tibradden Mountain

Route 25: Cruagh Mountain Loop

Route 26: Massy's Wood

Route 27: Hell Fire Club

Route 28: Glenasmole Reservoirs Loop

Route 29: Ballymorefinn Hill and Seahan Circuit

Route 30: Saggart Hill

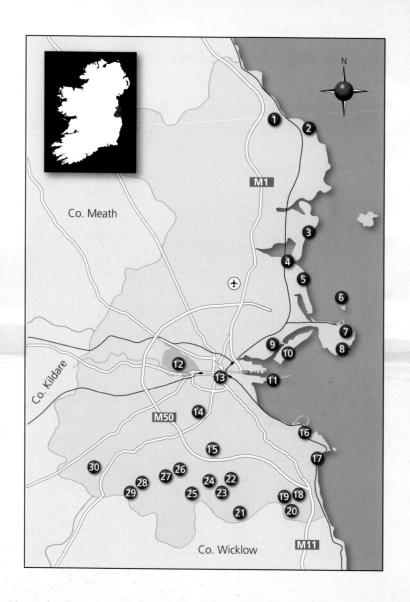

Co. Meath

Co. Kildare

Co. Wicklow

M1

M50

M11

N

Quick-Reference Route Table

No.	Route	Category
1	Ardgillan Castle, Park and Demesne	Park and woodland trail
2	Skerries *Slí na Sláinte*	Coastal and townland trail
3	Donabate Coastal Walks	
	Option 1: Donabate to Portrane Coastal Walk	Coastal trail
	Option 2: Donabate Beach and Burrow Estuary	Coastal trail and road
4	Malahide Marina, Estuary and Castle	Coastal, road and park trail
5	Portmarnock to Malahide Coastal Walk	Coastal and road trail
6	Ireland's Eye	Island trail
7	Howth Northern and Eastern Loop	Coastal and road trail
8	Howth Southern Loop	Coastal trail
9	St Anne's Park	Park and woodland trail
10	North Bull Island Loop	Coastal and mudflats trail
11	Irishtown Nature Park and Poolbeg Lighthouse	
	From Marine Drive Nature Park only	Park and coastal trail
	From Marine Drive Including Lighthouse	Park, coastal and lighthouse trail
	Nature Park from Shelly Banks car park	Park and coastal trail
	Lighthouse from Shelly Banks car park	Lighthouse trail
12	Phoenix Park	Park trail
13	Grand Canal and Dublin City Loop	Canal and road trail
14	Dodder River Walk and Bushy Park	Park, river and woodland trail
15	Marlay Park	Park and woodland trail
16	Sandycove Heritage Trail	Coastal and road trail
17	Dalkey Quarry and Killiney Hill Circuit	Hill trail
18	Rathmichael Woods Circuit	Hill and woodland trail
19	Lead Mines Chimney and Carrickgollogan	Hill and woodland trail
20	Barnaslingan Trail and The Scalp	Hill and woodland trail
21	Prince William's Seat and Raven's Rock from Glencullen	
	From Boranaraltry Bridge	Hillwalk and mountain trail
	From R116	Road, hillwalk and mountain trail
22	Three Rock Wood and Three Rock Mountain	
	from Ticknock Lower	Mountain trail
23	Fairy Castle, Two Rock Mountain and Three Rock Mountain from Ticknock Upper	
	Short Option	Hillwalk and mountain trail
	Long Option	Hillwalk and mountain trail
24	Tibradden Mountain	Mountain trail
25	Cruagh Mountain Loop	Hillwalk and mountain trail
26	Massy's Wood	Woodland trail
27	Hell Fire Club	Hillwalk and mountain trail
28	Glenasmole Reservoirs Loop	Valley and reservoir trail
29	Ballymorefinn Hill and Seahan Circuit	Hillwalk and forest trail
30	Saggart Hill	Hill and woodland trail

Introduction

O cool is the valley now
And there, love, will we go
For many a choir is singing now
Where Love did sometime go.
And hear you not the thrushes calling,
Calling us away?
O cool and pleasant is the valley
And there, love, will we stay.

– 'O Cool Is The Valley Now' by James Joyce (1882–1941)

Dublin is Ireland's capital city and its most populated county. The city and suburbs are a bustling and thriving urban metropolis with nearly 1.35 million people, making up nearly a third of Ireland's overall population.

The official Irish name for Dublin is *Baile Átha Cliath* which means 'town of the hurdled ford', referring to a bank of wooden hurdles built across the River Liffey by the medieval Vikings. However, the name Dublin really originates from two Irish words: *Dubh*, meaning 'black', and *Linn*, meaning 'pool'.

How it got its name is quite fascinating. For this, we have to step back in time and unlock the secrets of Dublin's most important, yet forgotten river. The Poddle River begins in the Cookstown area, north-west of Tallaght, then flows east, north-east, and ultimately into the Liffey in Dublin city centre. Today, its outlet into the Liffey is little more than an open sewer, locked behind a metal gate and ignored by thousands of passers-by along Wellington Quay.

The Poddle is the river of old Dublin. The city could not have expanded in bygone years if not for the freshwater supply of the Poddle, in contrast to the salty and undrinkable water of the Liffey. But the Poddle is hidden today: concreted over and driven underground.

During the reign of the Vikings in medieval times, the Poddle flowed into a dark tidal pool where the clear river water entered the Liffey. The Vikings founded a settlement there around AD 841 and named it *Dyflin*, from the Irish *Dubhlinn*, or 'Black Pool'. In later years the Black Pool was filled in. The site of *Dyflin* is where the Castle Gardens at Dublin Castle are today.

The Poddle River was crucial to the growth of the Viking settlement, both as a trading and defensive base. In fact, *Dyflin*, or *Dubhlinn*, was the commercial hub for the Vikings, similar to Dublin's International Financial Services Centre (IFSC) today. It was where the Vikings built their ships and repaired their sails, loaded and unloaded their goods, and traded slaves, gold and silver.

The bloody victory by Brian Boru and his troops over an army led by Mael Morda and Earl Sigurd at Clontarf on Good Friday 1014 marked the end of the Viking reign in Ireland. However, by this time the Vikings had already begun to be absorbed into and stamp their mark on Irish Celtic society. The Hiberno-Norse King of Dublin, Sigtrygg Silkbeard, for example, went on to found Dublin's famous Christ Church Cathedral in the city centre.

Following the end of the rule of Boru's grandson Muirchertach in 1119, Dublin fell to Strongbow and the Normans in 1170. The Anglo-Normans imposed control over Dublin until it was handed over to English parliamentary forces in 1647, which commenced a lengthy period of British rule until the Easter Rising 1916.

For over 1,000 years when Dublin was ruled by the Vikings, the Anglo-Normans and the English, three rivers – the Tolka, Liffey and Dodder – flowed into the Irish Sea, forming a broad marshy delta around Dublin Bay. But starting in the late eighteenth century, a process of land reclamation and natural silting has filled this delta, moving the development of the city inward.

Today, Dublin city is divided into the north and south side by the Liffey River. Two canals, the Royal Canal and the Grand Canal, form a ring around the city centre. The city and its suburbs are sheltered by the quartzite finger of Howth in the north and the granite uplands of Killiney Hill and the Dublin Mountains to the south. Beyond the city to the north are windswept beaches, historic castles, beautiful villages, rugged headlands and islands. To the south there are many hectares of unspoilt countryside and mountain vistas to discover.

The Dublin Mountains Way is a 43km (27-mile) waymarked trail which runs from Shankill in the east through the mountains and finishes at the Sean Walsh Memorial Park in Tallaght. The long-distance trail crosses a variety of landscapes, from conical Carrickgollogan and the broad moorland of Fairy Castle to the idyllic Glenasmole Valley. It passes the highest pub in County Dublin (Johnnie Fox's), an ancient tomb on Tibradden and the notorious Hell Fire Club building on Montpelier Hill.

The thirty routes in this guidebook will take you on a journey to some of County Dublin's finest landscapes and historical attractions. The routes are ordered in a general north-to-south direction, starting from the eighteenth-century Ardgillan Castle near Skerries to Saggart Hill which rises above the foothills of Rathcoole. In between, it explores some lovely beaches in north Dublin, an island, the headland of Howth, various city and suburban parks, part of the Grand Canal and many of the highlights of the Dublin Mountains Way.

Above all, the guidebook is a journey on foot that everyone in the family can enjoy. The walks range from around 1 to 5 hours in length. They are all fairly easy walks with no significantly steep ascent or descent.

The walks will take you across a variety of trails and footpaths within a park, through woods, along the coast or on a hill.

The routes in this book are handpicked to encourage people in Dublin who are not walkers to start the activity. It does not matter how old or how fit you are. The walks are also graded to suit children aged three, six, and ten years and above. They are also tailor-made to suit busy families who cannot afford to spend the entire day out walking.

There are also interesting stopping points to keep curious kids engaged, with tales of folklore, historical snippets and information on flora and fauna embedded within the route guide. The routes in this book will also be useful for families and visitors from outside of the Dublin area and tourists from abroad.

So as James Joyce puts it, 'O cool and pleasant is the valley' – so get outdoors, get walking, get exploring and get happy. I hope you share many enjoyable and memorable moments with your family and loved ones doing all the routes in this guidebook and discovering the very best County Dublin has to offer – happy hiking!

Using This Book

Maps

The maps in this guidebook are approximate representations of the routes only. For all Grade 2 and 3 routes in this guidebook, the use of detailed maps is recommended. A general knowledge of map reading and scale interpretation is useful for all routes in this book. For all upland routes in this book, and in particular the Grade 3 ones, basic map and compass skills are also recommended. For durability in wind and rain, it is suggested to photocopy and laminated the relevant section of the map to take with you on the walks. Especially relevant to the upland routes in this book, please note that forestry, tracks and waymarked trails may change from time to time, so get the latest editions of all maps.

The following maps are recommended for Grade 2 and 3 routes in this guidebook. Maps for Grade 1 routes are also listed, but since there are few to no navigational difficulties for these, the maps presented in this book should be sufficient for them.

- Ordnance Survey Ireland (OSi) 1:50,000 *Discovery Series* Sheet 43: **Routes 1 and 3**.
- Ordnance Survey Ireland (OSi) 1:50,000 *Discovery Series* Sheet 50: **Routes 3, 5, 6 to 8, 10, 18 and 19**.
- Ordnance Survey Ireland (OSi) 1:15,000 *Official Dublin City and District Street Guide* (ISBN 978-1-908852-54-0): **Routes 2, 4 to 17**.
- East West Mapping 1:30,000 *The Dublin Mountains & North Wicklow*: **Routes 15, 20 to 30**.

All maps may be purchased from most outdoor shops or online from: www.osi.ie or www.eastwestmapping.ie

Grid References

Grid references (e.g. **O 081**$_{23}$ **196**$_{98}$) provided in this book should help you plan a route and upload it to your GPS, or to use your GPS to check a grid reference. Set your GPS to use the Irish Grid (IG). Note that GPS units are precise to 5 digits, whereas a 3-digit precision will usually suffice using map and compass, and hence these are outlined in **bold**.

Walking Times

Walking times in this book are calculated based on individual speeds of somewhere between 2 to 3km per hour, taking into account walking speeds of young children, especially from three to ten years. One minute has also been added for every 10m of ascent so, for example, if a height gain of 150m is the case, then 15 minutes have been added to the total walking time. A 6km walk with a total of 150m ascent will take approximately 2¼ to 3¼ hours. In some routes, I have also added time for the difficulty or length of terrain.

Note that the 'Time' stated in the routes of this guidebook does not include the additional time required for stops, lunch, drinks and photography.

Metric and imperial units are given for the summary at the start of the route for 'Distance' and 'Ascent'. All heights of summits are also given in metric and imperial units. However, elsewhere in the text only metric distances and heights are given.

Walk Grades

Walks in this book are graded 1 to 3 based on *level of difficulty*, with 1 being the easiest and 3 the hardest. Note that in winter under snow and ice conditions, all Grade 3 routes are unsuitable for young children. All Grade 3 routes require hiking boots with good ankle support – two-season ones are fine and these can be used at any time of the year apart from winter. You can get away with a good pair of runners for all Grade 1 routes. For a summary of footwear for all the routes see the Quick-reference Route Table on pp 8–9.

Grade 1:   Suitable for adult beginners and children aged three years and above. These routes are on canal, coastal, hill, mudflats, park, river, road, townland or woodland trails with good and firm underfoot conditions. There are few to no navigational difficulties as the routes are generally easy or signposted throughout. Grade 1 routes involve distances of up to 7km in length, negligible or up to 100m height gain, and are up to 3½ hours long. The exception to this rule is Route 6: Ireland's Eye (2.5km, 90m), which has been assigned Grade 2 due to its distance from the mainland, terrain and ruggedness of the walk.

Grade 2:   Suitable for adult beginners and children aged six years and above. These routes are generally on formal trails or well-graded, constructed paths with good underfoot conditions. However, there may be some sections of open countryside or slightly rougher ground. The routes are generally signposted, but there may be sections with no signs. Grade 2 routes involve distances of up to 9km in length, up to 210m height gain and are up to 4¼ hours long.

Grade 3: Suitable for adults with basic hillwalking experience and children aged ten years and above. There may be some formal and signposted paths but generally these routes involve informal paths and slightly rougher ground on open mountainside. Basic map and compass navigational skills in all weather conditions are also recommended. Grade 3 routes involve distances of up to 11km in length, up to 360m height gain and are up to 5½ hours long.

Responsible walking

Take nothing but pictures, leave nothing but footprints, kill nothing but time.

Always use gates and stiles where available. If a gate is closed, close it after entering. If it is open, leave it open. If you cannot open a closed gate to enter, go over at its hinge with care. Take care not to damage any gates, stiles or fences.

When parking, be considerate not to block any gates, farm-access lanes or forest entrances as local residents, farm machinery and emergency services may need access at all times.

Note that landowners generally do not approve of dogs being brought onto their property, and this includes their land on the open hillside. If you must take your dog, ask the landowner's permission: this especially applies to Routes 21 and 29. This, of course, doesn't apply to public roads or public parks. If you need to bring your dog on upland trails other than Routes 21 and 29, keep it on a leash. Note also it will not be practical to bring your dog on Route 6 (Ireland's Eye).

Leave No Trace (www.leavenotraceireland.org) is an outdoor ethics programme designed to promote and inspire responsible outdoor recreation through education, research and partnerships. Put its ethics into practice, even if there is no one about to see you do it.

- Take out all litter including biodegradable materials, such as apples cores, orange peel and food scraps.
- Do not disturb structures and artifacts such as old walls and hilltop cairns, and treat another's property as your own.
- Leave all natural wildlife habitats as they are, such as fallen trees and wildflowers.
- Minimise the effect of fire as it could lead to uncontrolled wildfires and charred park benches.
- Stick to established trails to prevent upland and trail erosion and never feed farm animals or wildlife.

Equipment for you and for your children

It is recommended to carry waterproofs/windproofs (jacket and over-trousers) and a basic first-aid kit for all routes in this book. The first-aid kit would consist of items such as plasters, sterile wipes, small bandages and sterile water pods. Two-season hiking boots with good ankle support, a fleece top, walking trousers, gloves, socks, hat, food and drink are also recommended for all coastal, hill and mountain routes in this book. You may also wish to include some sun cream and midge repellent in the summer, especially for hill and mountain routes.

A few tips to bear in mind when taking children especially on Grade 2 or 3 routes:

- **Bring sufficient warm clothes and waterproofs**, and a spare fleece for kids: children have a smaller surface area for their body size and heat up or cool down quicker than adults. A group shelter is also great for kids to get into, especially on windy days in exposed areas on the hill or coast.
- **Bring extra fluids:** children have higher fluid requirements per kilo of body weight compared to adults. As a simple rule of thumb, if you need 500ml of fluid for yourself, then you need to bring a similar amount of fluid for each child.
- **Bring extra snacks:** these are a useful distraction especially for young children when a little encouragement is required. Children tend to eat little and often rather than having one large meal. Healthier foods and drinks such as sandwiches, fresh fruit, cereal bars and no-added-sugar squashes are recommended. The occasional treat such as some sweets, a chocolate bar or hot chocolate in a flask might not do any harm.
- **Make it fun:** involve children in activities during the walk such as putting together a checklist of things to discover or find, taking pictures on the route and checking out your destination on the map. Reward them for reaching the summit!
- **Always have a back-up plan:** for different reasons things might not work out on the day, for example if the weather turns bad. Restless participants will make the experience memorable for the wrong reasons. Therefore don't be afraid to turn back, retrace your steps and return on a better, sunnier day.

One piece of advice is never to wear jeans on a walk. Jeans are not suitable because when they get wet, they stay soaked and retain water next to your skin, increasing the risk of hypothermia. This risk is accentuated for children.

A toddler backpack carrier is recommended for children aged from six months to three years for all the routes in this book. A backpack carrier is more efficient than a buggy, will free up your arms and will suit all terrain and places where there are steps. Framed carriers are preferred to unframed ones. Although more expensive, framed carriers have better weight distribution, are more comfortable and robust, and offer a more elevated position for your child. The Osprey Poco Premium is great investment but Little Life and Deuter brands are good too.

Outdoor Safety

1. Do not solely rely on the use of GPS. Map and compass skills are recommended.
2. Get a detailed weather forecast.
3. There is a temperature drop of 2 to 3ºC for every 300m of ascent. If it is a pleasant morning at sea level it could be cold on the summit of Seahan. The wind is around 25 per cent stronger at 500m than it is at sea level. Wind velocities at a col/saddle are higher and wind effects can be strong on an exposed ridge.
4. In case of emergency call 999/112 and ask for 'Mountain Rescue'. Before dialling, it helps to be ready to give a grid location of your position.
5. Keep well away from cliff edges, especially on coastal routes. Be cautious of wet or slippery rock, holes in the ground on vegetated slopes and slippery tree roots in the forest and woodlands.
6. Ensure that you, your clothing and equipment are up to the task for yourself and your children, and know the limitations of all. Winter conditions require specialised gear.
7. Be aware of the daylight hours over the time of year. Most accidents happen during descent or near the end of the day. Carry enough emergency equipment (e.g. a head torch, group shelter and spare batteries) should an injury occur and you need to stop moving.
8. It is recommended not to walk alone, except in areas where there are other people around. Leave word with someone responsible.
9. Do not leave any valuables in cars. Keep all things in the boot and out of sight to avoid unwanted attention. There is a high incidence of theft from car parks in the Dublin Mountains, even on busy weekends. Report all thefts and suspicious activity to the Gardaí.
10. Carry a fully charged mobile phone, but keep it well away from the compass as its needle gets affected by metal.

Useful Contacts

Emergencies Dial 999 or 112 for emergency services, including mountain rescue and coastguard.

Weather Useful sources of information are www.met.ie, www.mountain-forecast.com and www.yr.no. The rainfall radar on www.met.ie is particularly useful. You may also call 1550 123 851 for a detailed five-day Leinster forecast using Met Éireann Weatherdial, a premium-rate weather service.

Tourist Information For tourist information go to www.visitdublin.com or visit the Discover Ireland tourist offices at 25 Suffolk Street, Dublin 2 or 14 Upper O'Connell Street, Dublin 1. There are also Discover Ireland information offices in the arrival halls at Terminals 1 and 2 in Dublin Airport. If you wish to speak with someone directly, telephone (from within Ireland) 1890 324 583.

Transport The recommended and easiest mode of transport for all routes in this book is by car, especially if you have young children in the group. However, some routes are accessible by bus (Routes 9 to 15), train/DART (Routes 2 to 7, 11, 13 and 16) and LUAS (Routes 12 and 13). You need to factor in the additional walking distance from the drop-off point to the start of the walk if using public transport. Bus services within and around Dublin city and its suburbs are operated by Dublin Bus. See www.dublinbus.ie for latest bus numbers, current timetables or call +353 (0)1 873 4222 (8.30 a.m. – 6 p.m. Monday to Saturday excluding public holidays). For DART rail services see www.irishrail.ie/dart. For LUAS light rail tram services, see luas.ie. For intercity train services contact Irish Rail see www.irishrail.ie for latest timetables or call +353 (0)1 836 6222 (8.30 a.m. – 6 p.m. Monday to Friday excluding public holidays). If you need to book a taxi for transport in the Dublin Mountains, a useful contact is Glendalough Cabs, **mobile:** +353 (0)87 972 9452, **email:** glendaloughcabs@hotmail.com

Forest Service Forestry plantations in Ireland are managed by Coillte, the semi-state forestry company. For more information on forest recreation sites and trails see www.coillteoutdoors.ie All forest recreation area car park opening hours in this book were checked in 2016, but if there is any doubt, check www.dublinmountains.ie/recreation_sites or email: info@dublinmountains.ie

Waymarked trails For information on long-distance walking trails accessible from Dublin see: www.dublinmountains.ie/dublin_mountains_way/dublin_mountains_way and www.wicklowway.com

Access and Training Mountaineering Ireland, the representative body for walkers and climbers in Ireland, works to secure continued access and to provide walkers and climbers the opportunity to improve their skills. Tel: +353 (0)1 6251115; www.mountaineering.ie

Hillwalking Resource www.mountainviews.ie is a great hillwalking resource and provides mountain lists, comments and information.

Get Ireland Walking (www.getirelandwalking.ie) is a national initiative that aims to maximise the number of people participating in walking for health, wellbeing and fitness.

Irish Trails (www.irishtrails.ie) is a website from the National Trails Office which was established in 2007 by the Irish Sports Council to coordinate and drive the implementation of an Irish Trails Strategy, and to promote the use of recreational trails in Ireland. There are currently over 880 trails listed in the website.

Ardgillan Castle, Park and Demesne

An easy walk in lovely parklands overlooking the Irish Sea, with the added attractions of a walled garden, rose garden and an eighteenth-century castle.

Grade:	1
Distance:	3.5km (2¼ miles)
Ascent:	70m (230ft)
Time:	1½–2 hours
Map:	OSi 1:50,000 Sheet 43, or map of the demesne on: ardgillancastle.ie

Start/finish: Leave the M1 at Junction 5. Take the R132 to Balrothery. Follow signs for 'Ardgillan Castle' or 'Ardgillan Park' at Balrothery. There is a car park with ample spaces in the grounds of the castle at **O 218**85 **606**67.

Ardgillan is derived from the Irish *Ard Choill* meaning 'high wood' and understandably so. Its 81-hectare (*c.* 200-acre) demesne is perched on an elevated slope overlooking the Irish Sea giving views of the north Dublin coastline as far-reaching as the Mourne Mountains in County Down. The demesne itself is a mixture of wild woodland, green meadows, rolling lawns, a walled garden, rose garden, playground and sheltered picnic areas. It is difficult not to notice Ardgillan Castle, a large two-storey country-style house with turrets and castellated embellishments, as you enter the parklands. Originally named Prospect House, its central section was built in 1738 by Rev. Robert Taylor, the grandson of Thomas Taylor who came to Ireland to work with the Irish Commission on the Down Survey in the 1650s. The castle's west and east wings were added in the late eighteenth century. The Taylor family remained at Ardgillan for over 200 years until finally selling the estate to Heinrich Potts in 1962. Ardgillan was bought by Dublin County Council in 1982, and is now under the ownership of Fingal County Council. There is a traditional Irish tearoom located off the main reception area of the castle. Castle tours are also available on demand. For more information and opening times of the park and castle see: ardgillancastle.ie

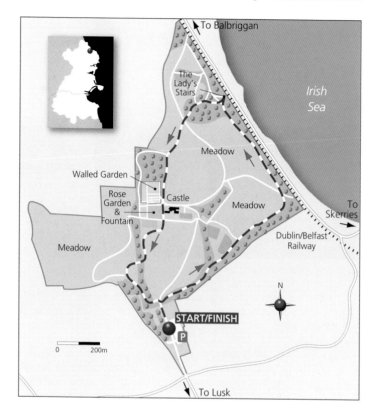

Route Description

There are fine views of the islands off the coast of Skerries to the east from the car park. The lighthouse on Rockabill and the distant profile of the Mourne Mountains can also be seen on a clear day.

Walk to the information board at the rear of the car park and follow the signs for 'Playground'. A tarmac footpath at a green area leads to a T-junction. Take a surfaced track to the right before the T-junction, following signs that say: 'Adventure Playground This Way'.

The track meanders under the cover of holly, oak and birch trees to reach a large playground on the left. The playground is coloured and themed on the castle and the sea. There are junior (two to six years) and senior (six to twelve years) areas with over thirty pieces of play equipment for the kids.

If not visiting the playground, continue ahead on a footpath that meanders beside a large green meadow to your left. There are picnic tables and wooden benches should you need them.

21

Playground at Ardgillan Park.

Follow the broad surfaced and stony footpath down to a bend, keeping the green meadow always to your left. The footpath is bordered by trees on the right, and the sea can be seen ahead as it descends to the bend.

Just after the bend, the path forks. Take the right fork to follow a footpath that runs parallel to the road and DART line, which is hidden behind the trees to your right. The path is uneven in places and soon enough Ardgillan Castle can be seen at the top of a green meadow away to the left.

Shortly after going under the cover of trees, the path reaches a three-way junction. A footbridge known as the Lady's Stairs leads over the DART line and the road. Built by the railway company in the 1840s, the footbridge provided the Taylor family with access to the beach in their heyday.

Here, take the leftmost junction, following signs for 'Gardens', 'Ice House' and 'Castle & Tea Room'. Ignore the next junction on the right and continue along the uneven path to emerge from the trees.

There is another three-way junction here and Ardgillan Castle can again be seen away to the left. Continue straight ahead, with the large green meadow (and coastline) to your left.

At the next set of junctions, continue ahead, following signs for 'Castle & Tea Rooms'. Follow the tree-lined footpath, which gradually rises to a junction with a walled garden to your right.

The walled garden is worth a visit. There are bergenias, lupins, fuchsia, anemone and more exotic plants such as the *Rubiaceae Coprosma Nitida* from New Zealand and the *Myrtaceae Callistemon Pallidus* from Tasmania.

22

Squirrels can often be seen in the grounds of the gardens. Gooseberry, apple, raspberry, white currant and cherry trees can also be found in the gardens as well as a vegetable plot which has artichoke, cabbage, rhubarb, runner beans, tomato, celery, turnip and spinach beet.

Head back out of the walled garden and continue ahead to visit Ardgillan Castle and its tearooms, or to take a castle tour. When done, retrace steps back to the walled garden. Go left there and, with the castle on your left, follow the footpath to reach the rose garden.

Entrance to the walled garden.

Turn right to enter the rose garden, if you wish to visit it. If not, continue ahead to a gap in a stone wall that provides access to a large green meadow. Take the footpath leading uphill. As you gain height, look back at the fine views of Ardgillan Castle with the sea as a backdrop.

The footpath veers right at a bend and goes under a canopy of branches to emerge into an open green area. Turn left at a junction and follow the footpath to arrive back at the junction with the 'Adventure Playground This Way' sign encountered at the start of the walk.

Turn right there and head back to the car park.

Ardgillan Castle from the footpath leading uphill beyond the stone wall after the rose garden.

Skerries *Slí na Sláinte*

Enjoy the best of the charming seaside town of Skerries on foot.

Grade:	1
Distance:	4km (2½ miles)
Ascent:	Negligible
Time:	1½–2 hours
Map:	OSi 1:15,000 *Official Dublin City* and *District Street Guide*

Start/finish: Leave the M1 at Junction 4. Take the R132 exit, then the R127 to Lusk. Continue along the R127 to reach Skerries town. Continue onto Thomas Hand Street/R128 to reach a roundabout. Take the first exit at the roundabout onto Strand Street, then shortly after, veer right onto Harbour Road. Pass Skerries Harbour on the left and continue for around 500m before veering right into the Red Island car park at **O 256**₆₇ **612**₀₀ at the sea front.

Skerries, or *Na Sceirí*, in Irish originates from the Norse word *sceir* meaning 'reef' or 'rocky islands'. The town has been inhabited since 5000 BC as evident from Neolithic stone axes and flint tools found here. On his return as a Christian missionary, it was also the site of St Patrick's first settlement in Ireland after he was banished by the Wicklow natives at the mouth of the River Inver-dea, now called the Vartry. It became well known in the sixteenth century for its milling industry, then later in the eighteenth century for its thriving fishing industry. Today, it is an attractive seaside town for Dubliners to escape from the city for a stroll along the beach, a round of golf, or for a taste of water sports. Our route follows the Skerries *Slí na Sláinte* meaning 'path of health'. This is a waymarked route developed by the Irish Heart Foundation, which is 4km in length and marked by colourful signposts situated at 1km intervals. This delightfully easy route has many attractions which include islands, sandy beaches, a Martello tower, windmills and a memorable ice-cream stop at the end!

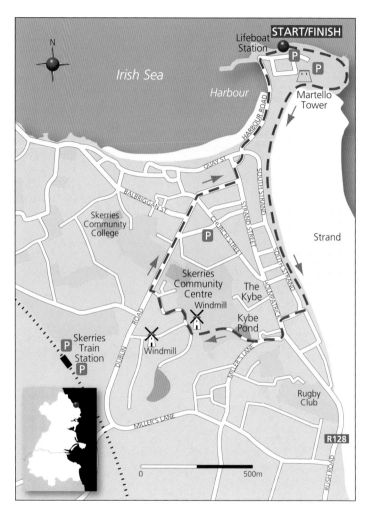

Route Description

Red Island is actually a small peninsula to the north of Skerries town, shaped like a camel's head. At the car park, follow a tarmac footpath with the sea to your left. The route is marked with *Slí* signposts. Wooden benches are installed at regular intervals along the footpath. A large green footprint is painted on the tarmac footpath. This is probably after a local legend that tells of St Patrick taking two giant strides to the mainland to confront the local people about a missing goat, and leaving an impression of this footprint on a rock.

Slí na Sláinte *signposts and footprint marks on the footpath at the Red Island car park point the way forward.*

The Skerries islands of Colt, St Patrick's, Shenick's and Rockabill with its lighthouse can be seen out to sea. These islands are Special Protection Areas (SPAs) and Special Areas of Conservation (SACs) for wildlife. Colt Island is a breeding ground for mallard, shelduck, ringed plover and the eider duck. Shenick's Island is an important roosting site from autumn to spring for thousands of birds such as the brent goose, turnstone, curlew and oystercatcher. Rockabill has the largest colony of roseate terns in north-west Europe, which breed on the island from spring to early autumn.

St Patrick's Island (*Inis Pádraig*) has up to 1,000 pairs of cormorants and up to 100 grey seals from the winter to early spring. The island is also said to be the landing site of St Patrick after he was sent as a missionary to Ireland by Pope Celestine in 431. He founded a monastery there, which was later burned by the Vikings in 797. In 1148, a synod of over 200 priests and bishops, spearheaded by St Malachy, gathered on the island to discuss issues regarding the Celtic Church and its practices. Ruins of a twelfth-century church, monastic buildings and a tomb shrine can be found on the island today.

The footpath swings round towards a Martello tower on a rise above. The tower was installed in the early nineteenth century with 24-pounder guns which were never fired. When the Napoleonic Wars ended, the tower was used by the coastguard, by a family and finally as an entertainment complex. The tarmac footpath passes under the Martello tower then turns left to run along the strand. A section of the strand, reputed to be the warmest part of the beach, is known locally as 'The Ovens'. There were bathing booths here in the 1900s.

Continue on the footpath or along the beach for around 800m to reach a metal footbridge. Cross the footbridge over a brook then turn right at a wooden bench and head inland. After a stone footbridge, continue ahead on to Brookville Lane to reach a T-junction.

The Malting House Inn, a traditional Irish pub built in 1870, lies across

Martello tower at the Red Island car park near Skerries Beach.

the street. Go left there at the T-junction. At the next junction turn right, following *Slí na Sláinte* signs into Miller's Lane, and soon pass Holmpatrick Church. The church dates back to 1220 when Archbishop Henry de Londres transferred the monastery on St Patrick's Island to the mainland. *Holm* is an ancient Norse word meaning a 'small island near the mainland' or an Old Danish word meaning 'harbour', so it is hardly surprising the church was named Holmpatrick.

Shortly after the church, still following signs for *Slí na Sláinte*, turn right into Skerries Mills. Pass the Kybe Pond on the right where mute swans can usually be seen gracing its waters, which is fed by natural underground springs.

A lane leads into a car park with the Skerries windmills perched on a grassy mound ahead.

The Great Windmill originally had four sails. However, after a fire destroyed it in 1844, the more efficient five-sail variant was built. The windmill's stone tower is 15m high with a sail diameter of 20m. There is a Visitor Centre there which includes a water wheel, mill race, tearooms and a craft shop.

Holmpatrick Church.

Windmill at Skerries Mills.

There is a broad, surfaced footpath running below the windmills. Follow this footpath, keeping some sports pitches away to your right. The footpath gradually rises to the Martine Court housing estate. Turn right at a stone pillar and follow signs for *Slí na Sláinte*.

Follow the housing estate road as it bends left and is flanked by houses. Go through a gap in the wall before veering left out of the estate and onto the Dublin road. There are *Slí* arrows on the lamp post.

Turn right onto the Dublin road, passing a Texaco service station on the left and the Skerries community centre to your right. Continue straight ahead into Skerries town to reach a monument at the roundabout. Take the first exit at the roundabout onto Strand Street. Shortly after, veer right onto Harbour Road to pass Skerries Harbour and its pier to the left.

The pier dates from 1496 and the harbour was once the port of a thriving fishing industry which peaked in 1784. If you wish, leave the road and walk along the beach to admire the colourful boats and yachts that decorate its waters. The beach also has a potpourri of colourful pebbles and seashells. Look out for periwinkles and shore crabs too.

Back on Harbour Road, pass Skerries Sailing Club, some bars and restaurants before arriving back at Red Island car park at the start. Just before the car park, be sure to treat yourself to some delicious home-made ice cream at Storm in a Teacup (open seven days a week from May to October).

Skerries harbour and pier.

Donabate Coastal Walks

Explore the best sections of Donabate's fine coastline and enjoy views out to Lambay Island.

Option 1: Donabate to Portrane Coastal Walk

Grade:	1
Distance:	3.25km (2 miles)
Ascent:	Negligible
Time:	1¼–1¾ hours
Map:	OSi 1:50,000 Sheets 43 and 50

Option 2: Donabate Beach and Burrow Estuary

Grade:	1
Distance:	4km (2½ miles)
Ascent:	Negligible
Time:	1½–2 hours
Map:	OSi 1:50,000 Sheet 50

Start/finish: Leave the M1 at Junction 4. Take the R126 exit for Donabate. Pass the entrance for Newbridge Demesne along the R126 and continue to Donabate. After a sharp right-hand bend you will see a large red-brick church. Leave the R126 before it bends again and head straight ahead along a minor road, following signs for Corballis (L2170) or Donabate Beach. Pass a golf club and continue to the end of the road. There is a new car park before the Waterside House Hotel. If you are staying or eating at the hotel, there are spaces to park there too at **O 251**40 **492**86.

Donabate comes from the Irish word *Domhnach Bat* meaning 'the church of the boat or ferry'. *Domhnach* is often used for churches or areas with strong links to Ireland's patron saint, Patrick. The hammerhead-shaped peninsula of Donabate is tucked between the Rogerstown Estuary to the north and Broadmeadow/Burrow estuary to the south. In 1912, Donabate had a population of only 734 living in 150 houses, but this has grown to over 5,500 people today. This route explores two easy walking options from the Waterside House Hotel by Donabate Beach. One is a there-and-back coastal path to Portrane in the north, and the other is an inland route towards the Burrow Estuary before an approach to Donabate Beach via an access path through a golf course.

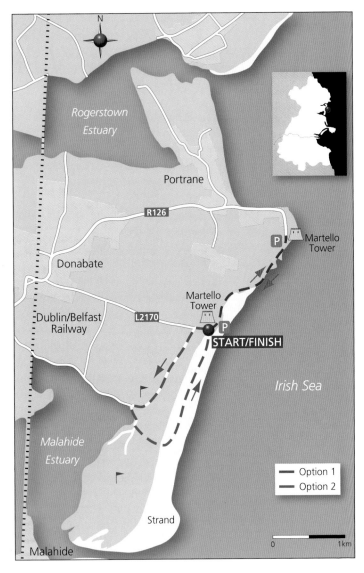

Route Description

Option 1: Donabate to Portrane Coast Walk

There are public toilets to the left of the Martello tower by the hotel. The Martello tower, around 12m in height and diameter, is one of many around

The coastal footpath from Donabate to Portrane, with the red-bricked buildings of St Ita's Hospital ahead.

Ireland built in the early 1800s during Napoleonic times.

A surfaced footpath to the left of the toilets swings around to pass the hotel on its left. A well-defined sandy footpath runs along the coast. It is impossible not to notice the long, flat shape of Lambay Island out to sea. The island lies around 4km offshore from the Martello tower at Portrane Quay, our turn-back point on this walk.

With an area of around 2.5km², Lambay is the largest island off Ireland's east coast. It western shoreline is tame compared to the more precipitous nature of its northern and eastern reaches. Its highest point, Knockbane, is a mere 126m/413ft. The name Lambay (Irish: *Reachrainn*) originates from the Old Norse *Lamb-ey* meaning 'lamb island', which probably stemmed from the tradition of shipping ewes to the island in the spring to lamb. The Irish name for Portrane, *Port Reachrainn*, originated from its position facing Lambay Island and means 'the port of Rechru'.

The shoreline is craggy and lined with contorted rocks dating back to the Ordovician period around 460 million years ago. But the coastal path makes it all very pleasant underfoot. After you pass a block of seaside cottages, some red-brick buildings appear ahead, along with a clock tower and a round tower. The round tower, unmarked as a historical monument, was commissioned in the nineteenth century by Mrs Sophia Evans (née Parnell, a great-aunt of Charles Stewart Parnell) of Portrane House in memory of her husband, George, who died in 1842. Both Sophia and her husband are buried in the grounds of St Catherine's church nearby.

The path soon passes a red-brick shelter sprayed with graffiti on the left. There is a subsidiary path leading away from the coast here and into

31

Martello tower and Tower Bay Beach at Portrane with Lambay Island out to sea.

the grounds of the red-brick buildings, which is actually St Ita's Hospital. Do not attempt to wander into these grounds as they are on private land.

The path soon runs along a stone wall enclosing a broccoli farm on the left. At the end of the wall, a fence safeguards a steep drop from the top of cliffs on the seaward side. Views towards the round tower beyond some fields to the left are best from around here.

The coastal path meanders above a rocky and craggy inlet before reaching the large car park at Tower Bay Beach in Portrane. There is another Martello tower here and Lambay Island can once again be seen out to sea.

A bit more on Lambay now, as you take in the fine views. The island, still privately owned by the Baring family trust, is accessible by invitation only. The Hon. Cecil Baring purchased the island for £5,250 in 1904 as an abode for him and his young wife, Maude Lorillard, the first American owner to win the Epsom Derby. The British architect Sir Edwin Lutyens converted a sixteenth-century fort on the island into a castle with a quadrangle, roofs of Dutch pantiles, an enceinte and bastioned gateway. Lutyens also designed the curved-step terraced harbour and White House, and renovated an old chapel on the island.

Lambay Island also supports a large colony of seabirds with thousands of herring gulls, common guillemots, kittiwakes and razorbills. There are also smaller numbers of Manx shearwaters, puffins and greylag geese there. Besides seabirds, there are grey seals, farmed cattle, fallow deer and even a small herd of red-necked wallabies on the island!

When ready, retrace steps back to the Waterside House Hotel at Donabate.

Burrow Estuary.

Option 2: Donabate Beach and Burrow Estuary

From the Waterside Hotel or the new car park, walk back along the L2170 towards a roundabout. Turn left at the roundabout, following signs for Corballis Golf Club. The road runs along the golf course on the left and is dotted with houses.

Another golf club, Balcarrick, appears on the right and Hands Mobile House Park is passed on the left. The road soon reaches a junction on the left with the Burrow Estuary directly ahead. Go left at the junction, following signs for Island Golf Club.

With the estuary away to your right, follow the road for some 350m before leaving it at **O 241**15 **479**93. A narrow path, signposted by a 'No Horses or Motorised Vehicles Beyond This Point' plate, passes through low shrubs and bushes.

The path, flanked by fences, soon becomes earthen before turning grassy. It enters the golf course at the corner of a fence near the eighth hole. At this point, the path becomes sandy again. Follow right-of-way signs through the golf course, and across the sixth hole.

The signs lead to a path at **O 244**21 **476**83 running down a sandy slope to Donabate Beach at marram-grass-covered sand dunes. The root system of the marram grass protects the dunes, prevening the sand being blown away by wind.

Turn left and walk along the beach, which runs below the golf course on the landward side. The small island of Ireland's Eye can be seen out to

Right-of-way signs at Island Golf Club.

sea. Keep an eye for rock pools along the beach, especially when the tide is out. Interesting sea creatures such as the Acorn Barnacle, Common Starfish, Shore Crab and mussels are commonly found at rock pools.

Continue along the beach to reach the Martello tower by the Waterside Hotel at the start.

Newbridge Demesne

Opened as a County Dublin Regional Park in 1986, the 150-hectare (370-acre) Newbridge Demesne is well worth a visit on the way back from Donabate. The park, designed by Wexford gardener Charles Fritzell in the eighteenth century, has a range of family attractions such as a traditional farm, a deer park, a limekiln, the ruins of Lanistown Castle and a children's playground. The centrepiece of the desmesne is Newbridge House, a 1736 Georgian mansion built by Archbishop Charles Cobbe. Delicious home-made food and tearooms are located in the Peacock Cafe at the house.

ROUTE 4:

Malahide Marina, Estuary and Castle

Enjoy the best of Malahide, from its marina and estuary to its castle and gardens. But be warned, there are plenty of shops to distract you!

Grade:	1
Distance:	5.75km (3½ miles)
Ascent:	Negligible
Time:	2–3 hours
Map:	OSi 1:15,000 *Official Dublin City and District Street Guide*

Start/finish: Malahide DART Station car park. If driving, you may pay at the station or by using the 'Park by text' facility. The cost at the time of writing was €4 per day. Note that the opening hours of Malahide Castle, Gardens and Park are 8 a.m. – 5 p.m. Monday–Friday and 9 a.m. – 5 p.m. at the weekend.

Malahide has had its fair share of ancient settlers from the Vikings (AD 795), Danes (AD 897) and Normans (1185). Its Irish equivalent *Mullach Íde* means 'sandhills of the Hydes', and is named after a Norman family in the area. In the early nineteenth century, Malahide was a hotspot for local visitors and foreign tourists with the arrival of its railway (1844), the opening of the Grand Hotel (1835) and the development of its Sea Baths. Its harbour was also used to import coal, timber and other goods. The area soon came to be known as 'Yellow Walls' from the stain that was left behind on its walls by the flax or linseed, which was grown locally. Starting from Malahide DART station, this route initially wanders through its village where it might be difficult to resist the temptation to visit one (or more!) of its many shops, boutiques, cafes and restaurants. Later, leaving the village behind, we meander along Malahide Marina before looping back towards the village. But not for long, as the route veers off again to run along the estuary for just under a kilometre before heading back inland towards the Malahide Castle and Gardens.

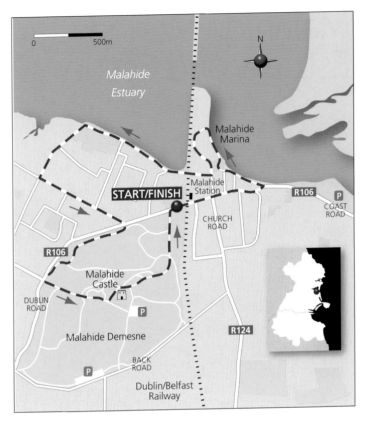

Route Description

Exit the DART station onto the Dublin Road. Turn left on the road and pass St Sylvester's Church on the left. Walk through Malahide village and continue along The Mall to reach some tennis courts on the left, with the Grand Hotel now to your right.

Leave the road here and turn left onto a tarmac footpath. The tennis courts are now above you to your left and the estuary appears to your right. On reaching a green square with a sculpture in its centre just before Siam Thai Restaurant, veer right onto a paved footpath.

This footpath runs along Malahide Marina, which is always packed with recreation boats, and soon passes under the Geisha restaurant. White's Laundry can be seen ahead. Veer left before the car park and follow a paved footpath as it traces an arc around the Marina Village Apartment blocks. The Malahide Railway, built in 1844 by Sir John McNeill, runs along a raised embankment to the right as the road swings around.

Malahide Marina.

The road is flanked by the apartment blocks as it goes under an arch, before it passes the Westbury Club and Casino on the right. At the crossroads by Starbucks at the corner, turn right to pass a fire station. Take a tarmac footpath to the left of the road under the arch of a bridge with a railway line now running above.

Cross the Bissett's Strand Road after the bridge and walk along a grassy stretch with the Malahide Estuary now stretching to your right. The estuary, which the Broadmeadow River flows into, is designated as a Special Protection and Conservation Area for wildlife. Its large expanse of open water and mudflats are the feeding grounds for hundreds of birds such as the mute swan, oystercatcher, gulls, curlew and mallard. Migratory birds such as the shelduck, godwit, redshank and brent goose also spend the winter here, before returning to their habitats in Canada and northern Europe. Its sheltered waters are also the spawning grounds for marine fish such as cod, herring and pollack.

Continue on the grassy and earthen footpath along the road for some 700m, passing many houses and the Wind & Wave Fingal Sailing School. The road veers left just before the Malahide Yacht Club. Cross the road with care here and follow the tarmac footpath to soon pass Pope John Paul II Primary School to the left.

After passing a housing estate the road rises gradually to reach a traffic light at a crossroads. Turn left here onto Yellow Walls Road and continue to a T-junction at the end of the road. Go left at the T-junction and after a few metres, cross the busy road at the traffic lights. Turn right and continue for another few metres before leaving the road and turning left into the grounds of Malahide Castle and Gardens.

Malahide Castle.

Once in the grounds, turn right and walk on a tarmac footpath keeping a large golf course to your left. The footpath soon bends left to reach a multiway junction. Veer right there to access another footpath, which runs under the cover of trees and parallel to a wall on the right. Continue until reaching a crossroads with the park entrance to your right. Ignore that and turn left there following signs for 'Castle Entrance', 'Playground' or 'Golf and Tennis'.

On reaching a T-junction, turn right and follow the 'Castle' trail which leads to a large green area on the right. Continue along the trail until Malahide Castle appears to your left. The castle is one of the oldest in Ireland and was home to the Talbot family from the twelfth century until the passing of the last Lord Talbot in 1973. But be warned! – the castle is said to be haunted by the ghost of Puck, one of Talbot's family servants.

Leave the green area and veer left to reach the front of the castle. You may visit the castle if you wish, but when ready follow a footpath to its right, which leads into a courtyard. There is an ancient fifteenth-century abbey, the resting place of generations of Talbots, to the right before the courtyard. The courtyard has shops to slow you further, such as Malahide Outdoor Store, Avoca Foodhall & Cafe and the Museum Shop.

Next, follow signs for 'Village and Marina' or 'DART Station' to the left of the courtyard entrance. The footpath runs by a high wall then exits through the main castle gates.

On reaching the main road, turn right and cross a bridge over the DART line. After you pass some brightly coloured houses, St Sylvester's Church comes into view. Cross the road at the traffic lights in front of the church and head back to the car park at the DART station.

ROUTE 5:

Portmarnock to Malahide Coastal Walk

Savour the coastal delights from Portmarnock to Malahide on foot in this point-to-point walk.

Grade:	2
Distance:	8km (5 miles)
Ascent:	Negligible
Time:	3–4 hours
Map:	OSi 1:50,000 Sheet 50 or OSi 1:15,000 *Official Dublin City* and *District Street Guide*

Start/finish: Malahide DART station car park. If driving, you may pay at the station or by using the 'Park by text' facility. The cost at the time of writing was €4 per day. From Malahide, take the DART southbound and come off at the next stop, Portmarnock. If travelling by DART from any other station, alight at Portmarnock DART station.

We explored Malahide – its village, shops, marina, its castle, park and gardens, and a section of its estuary – in the previous walk. This route takes in a popular coastal walking route that begins in Portmarnock, a seaside town to its south. Portmarnock (*Port Mearnóg*) is named after St Marnoch, a fifth-century Christian missionary who founded a church in the area. This is a point-to-point route from one DART station to another with plenty of highlights in between, including sandy Blue Flag beaches, a sculpture, towers, birdlife and wildflowers. Apart from a road walk inland at the start, this route is mainly a coastal trail on the beach or on a tarmac footpath. The distance of 8km can be quite demanding for younger children so if you need to cut the walk short there are bus stops along Strand Road that will whisk you back to Malahide. There is also a kiosk that sells ice creams and refreshments on the northern end of Velvet Strand, if needs must!

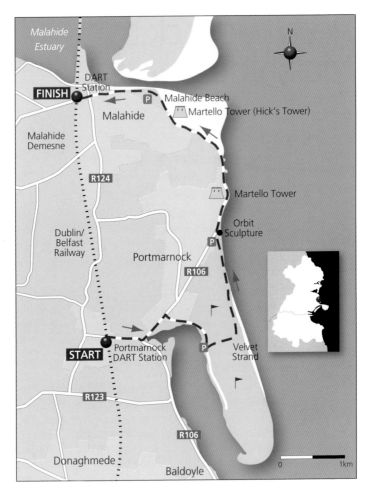

Route Description

Exit the DART station at Portmanock via the ramps to emerge on a road above. There is a bridge to your left and The Kilns Creche & Montessori ahead. Cross the road, then turn right onto its footpath. Pass The Links housing estate on your left and continue until reaching a small roundabout.

Turn left at the roundabout following signs for 'Port Beach Public Car Park'. Cross the busy road with care and continue to Portmarnock Bridge, which spans the Sluice River. Mallards are common on the grasslands and marshes along the riverside. Light-bellied brent geese can also be spotted here from September to May. These geese travel an astonishing 4,667km

Mallard and brent geese at the Sluice River.

from Arctic Canada, via Greenland and Iceland, to their winter roosting and feeding site here.

Continue on the footpath along the road to reach a junction with traffic lights by Staffords Funeral Home. Take a right there along the Golf Links Road following signs for Portmanock Golf Club. A grassy embankment to the right of the road meanders close to the Sluice River. Continue for around a kilometre to reach a public car park at **O 245**$_{35}$ **423**$_{28}$ on the left.

Turn left just before the car park and follow a broad grassy path that runs alongside a hedge to its left. Passenger planes can often be heard and seen flying overhead due to proximity to Dublin Airport. Old railway sleepers chart a course through marram-grass-covered sand dunes to

Looking along the Velvet Strand towards Portmarnock.

The Eccentric Orbit sculpture at Portmarnock.

emerge on Velvet Strand – one of County Dublin's finest beaches, which extends as a long finger of peninsula to the south-east of Portmarnock. The marram grass protects the dunes from erosion by the wind, tides and human trampling.

Turn left and stroll along the wide strand of sandy beach for just under 2km. As you approach its northern end, leave the beach and climb up tarmac steps. The steps lead up to a green metal gate which runs along low stone wall by Strand Road. There is an ice cream and refreshments kiosk (open March to October and not on rainy days, I was told!) just after the bus stop.

A few metres south of the kiosk is the Eccentric Orbit sculpture, defined by its globe axis and bronze needle. The needle points directly at the North Star, a navigation aid used for millennia. The sculpture commemorates a pioneering 33-hour flight across the Atlantic from Velvet Strand to Harbour Grace, Newfoundland in June 1930. The plane was the *Southern Cross* – an Australian aircraft piloted by Sir Charles Smith along with three others.

Head back towards the kiosk from the sculpture and follow the coastal route, keeping the sea to your right. Veer right onto a tarmac footpath in front of the White Sands Hotel and head towards a Martello tower. Keep a lookout for cormorants which can be seen commonly perched on rocks out to sea.

The footpath now runs to the right of the Martello tower. After a broad lay-by used for parking on the road, you will pass Robswall Park on the left. Steps lead down to the pebbly beach if you choose to wander down to the water's edge. Benches are also in place if you need a rest!

The grass verges along the road and its low stone walls thrive with wildflowers such as the wild carrot (*Daucus carota*), knapweed (*Centaurea nigra*), lady's bedstraw (*Galium verum*), tufted vetch (*Vicia cracca*), pyramidal orchid (*Anacamptis pyramidalis*) and field scabious (*Knautia arvensis*).

Leave the coastal tarmac footpath just before Hick's Tower (also known as Robswall Tower) and descend a ramp down to Malahide Beach. Hick's Tower was originally a Martello tower before being redesigned by Frederick Hick in 1911 when he added a red conical roof with a weathervane at its apex.

The ramp leading down to Malahide Beach, with Hick's Tower to the left.

A sandy stretch of beach leads to Malahide Estuary. There are two sections of beach here, named Flat Rock and High Rock. High Rock is a dangerous section of beach, access to which is via a metal ladder and suitable only for competent swimmers. In contrast, Flat Rock is a wide, sheltered section of beach with rippled sand and shallow water, and popular with families and children.

Leave the beach when a large car park appears on your left. At the car park, veer right along a grassy stretch and head in the direction of Malahide. The grassy stretch ends opposite the Seabank Bistro and the Food Fayre & Cafe. Now follow a tarmac footpath, pass Coast Restaurant and the Grand Hotel on your left, then some tennis courts on your right.

Continue along the road into Malahide village. You will eventually reach St Sylvester's Church and arrive at Malahide DART station, your journey's end.

Ireland's Eye

A delightful off-coast adventure to a small, remote island with ancient ruins, impressive rock formations and thriving birdlife.	**Grade:** 2
	Distance: 2.5km (1½ miles)
	Ascent: 90m (295ft)
	Time: 2–3 hours with added time due to natu of terrain
	Map: OSi 1:50,000 Sheet 50 or OSi 1:15,000 *Official Dublin City and District Street Guide*

Start/finish: The East Pier of Howth Harbour in north Dublin. Howth can be reached by DART from Dublin city centre or by car along the R105 from the city centre/Clontarf. If coming via the M50, head along the R139 (formerly the N32/Malahide Road) and follow signs for Donaghmede, Baldoyle and Sutton before joining the R105 to Howth.

Ireland's Eye is an uninhabited island just over a kilometre off the coast of Howth in north Dublin. It is a small island with an area of 0.22km². During ancient Celtic times, the island was named after a woman called Eria. When the Vikings arrived they named it Eria's Ey, with 'Ey' stemming from the Norse word *Iyot* which means 'island'. Later, Eria was substituted with 'Erin', the Hiberno-English derivative of *Éireann*, the Irish word for Ireland. Boats trips to the island are operated by Ireland's Eye Ferries. Up-to-date departure times, prices, email and a contact number can be found on www.irelandseyeferries.com. At the time of writing, ferries depart from the East Pier of Howth Harbour. The southern profile of Ireland's Eye can be admired in full from midway along the pier. Note that Howth gets very busy, especially at weekends and during the summer, so allocate plenty of time to find parking around the harbour. Boots are recommended for this route due to the trackless and rugged terrain for much of the walk. The terrain also gives the short 2.5km walk its Grade 2 rating. This route is best reserved for a clear, dry and sunny day.

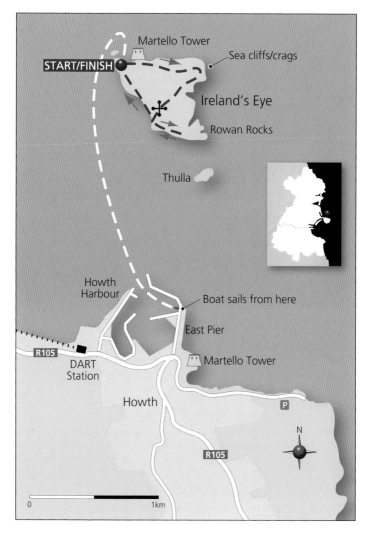

Route Description

During the short boat trip across the sea, keep a lookout for harbour porpoises and minke whales. The boat's landing point is on the north-west corner of Ireland's Eye in a small, rocky cove just below the Martello tower at **O 284**₅₅ **414**₈₆.

Step off the boat onto the island and ascend the seaweed-laced rocky steps with care, especially when they are wet. The Martello tower is one of

Ireland's Eye from the East Pier at Howth. Note the Martello tower on the left of the island, its highest point in the middle, and the cliff formation on its right. Lambay Island can be seen further in the distance.

many around Ireland built in the early 1800s to resist Napoleonic attacks. Its design and name 'Martello' is inspired by a fortified fortress at Mortella Point in Corsica. These towers are around 12m in height and diameter with an entrance above the ground.

Walk away from the Martello tower, keeping the sea to your left. A grassy and rocky ledge leads up and eastwards to the highest point on the island. All obvious difficulties can be bypassed to the left of the rocky slope, but keep well away from the cliff edge. If necessary, get your hands onto the rock along some sections for balance – but it is all very easy! Veer right near the summit to gain the top of Ireland's Eye at a mere 69m/226ft.

The view from the summit includes the Portmarnock coastline towards Malahide and Lambay Island to the north. It was in these waters near Lambay Island in March 1918 that the Howth trawler *Geraldine* was sunk by a German U-boat during a period known as the Fisherman's War. At the peak of the fishing industry in the 1970s, over 200 fishermen earned their living in these waters. Today, fishing is still a common activity and the catch includes black sole, cod, haddock, monkfish and prawns.

Descend eastwards from the summit and then traverse a grassy section towards the north-eastern end of the island. There are no paths

Boat landing point on Ireland's Eye near the Martello tower.

and the grass can be awkwardly long in the summer, but the ground is cushiony underfoot and should pose no problems if taken slowly.

After a short rise you will reach the edge of sea cliffs where you can admire a fang-like rock formation. According to legend, St Nessan fought the Devil from the rocks here to Howth and back again. The saint cast Satan off these cliffs where the rocks opened to swallow him.

The free-standing rock pinnacle here, known as The Stack, is home to seabirds such as cormorants, gulls, gannets and guillemots. The area is also a popular spot for rock climbers except during the seabird nesting season from April to July. Around twenty-eight climbing routes have been established here since the 1940s.

Looking back to the Martello tower and landing point from the summit of Ireland's Eye, with the Portmarnock coastline in the distance.

47

Walking through the ruins of an eighth-century chapel on Ireland's Eye.

From here, descend south-west for around 450m across grassy and vegetated terrain towards the ruins of an eighth-century chapel, Cill Mac Nessan, which can be clearly seen as you approach from the slopes above. Reach the roofless chapel at **O 287**47 **411**66 and go through a narrow gap to enter its ruins.

One of the oldest Irish manuscripts of the four Gospels, called The Garland of Howth, is said to have been penned by monks here. The illuminated manuscript was later brought to the mainland when the island suffered enemy attacks. Walk within the ruins of the chapel and exit via the arched doorway on its opposite end.

Follow an intermittent path to reach a sandy beach on the west side of the island. It is one of the few west-facing beaches on the east coast of Ireland. Go left and walk along the water's edge towards the southern end of the island. Go as far as you can and keep an eye out for grey seals, which are commonly found here. The seals breed on a tiny island to the south-east, called Thulla.

Retrace steps back to the beach and continue to its end. Leave the beach, veer right and ascend a sandy dune. A grassy stretch leads back towards the Martello tower, which soon comes into view.

Descend carefully down the rocky steps when the boat returns to collect you.

Howth Northern and Eastern Loop

A varied route along the harbour, clifftops and byways of a bustling seaside town.

Grade:	2
Distance:	7km (4¼ miles)
Ascent:	130m (426.5ft)
Time:	2¾–3¾ hours
Map:	OSi 1:50,000 Sheet 50 or OSi 1:15,000 *Official Dublin City* and *District Street Guide*

Start/finish: The large car park on the left just after Howth DART station. Howth can be reached by DART from Dublin city centre or by car along the R105 from the city centre/Clontarf. If coming via the M50, head along the R139 (formerly the N32/Malahide Road) and follow signs for Donaghmede, Baldoyle and Sutton before joining the R105 to Howth.

Howth is a craggy peninsula around 15km north-east of Dublin city. The area has been settled since Neolithic times and it has had several names over the centuries. Ptolemy called it *Edros* in his second-century map of Ireland. Its ancient Gaelic name was *Binn Eadair* (Hill of Eadair). Its English name – Howth – comes from the Norse word *Hoved* meaning 'headland'. Immortalised in James Joyce's *Ulysses*, the Howth of today is a tourist attraction by the sea. This route begins from the west end of Howth Harbour near the DART station. The harbour, built in the early nineteenth century by Scotsman Charles Rennie, provides safe anchorage to ships sailing to and from Holyhead. Harbour traffic increased as Howth became the mail station for Dublin in 1818. The route first meanders along the promenade, then passes the East Pier before snaking upward along Balscadden Road to reach a clifftop trail. Care should be taken along the clifftop section, especially when windy.

Route Description

Leave the car park and head eastwards along the promenade. Colourful boats and yachts are moored alongside the West Pier harbour to your left.

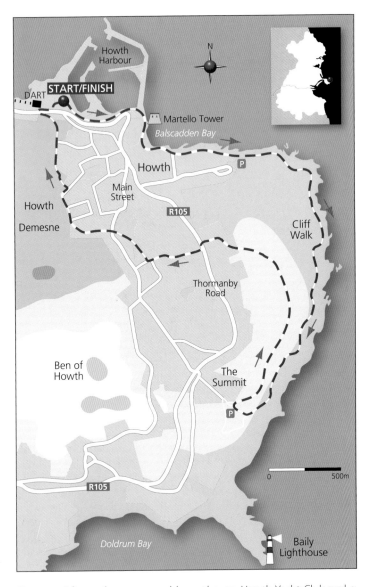

The paved footpath passes an old courthouse, Howth Yacht Club and a playground. The ruins of St Mary's Abbey, dating from the late fourteenth century, can also be seen on an elevated site away to the right.

The abbey is built on the site of the first church of Howth, which was founded by Sigtrygg, the King of Dublin, around 1042. The abbey's belfry once held bells that could be heard as far away as Lusk, around 20km to the north. In thick fog, the bells were rung to guide Howth fishermen back to the harbour.

The route soon passes Howth's East Pier. Here at noon on 26 July 1914, 1,500 rifles and 50,000 rounds of ammunition were smuggled in by Erskine Childers aboard his yacht, the *Asgard*. The

West Pier Harbour on Howth.

arms were later covertly distributed to 800 Irish volunteers who brought them into Dublin to be used during the 1916 Easter Rebellion.

Ireland's Eye, visited in the previous route, is visible across the sea to the left. A Martello tower, built during the Napoleonic Wars, sits atop a

Looking down on Balscadden Bay from the clifftop footpath above Puck's Rocks, with Howth Harbour and Ireland's Eye in the distance.

Clifftop footpath above Casana Rock, Piper's Gut and the Fox Hole at Howth.

grassy, eroded hillock to the right above some painted houses. At the King Sitric Fish Restaurant and Accommodation, the road veers right uphill.

Follow the road uphill to pass some houses on the left. When the road levels, peer down at the still waters of Balscadden Bay and admire far-reaching views of Ireland's Eye and Lambay Island.

On reaching Kilrock Road, ignore it and continue along a footpath by a stone wall to your left. You will soon reach Balscadden House – a white house with a dark blue door – on the left. The poet W.B. Yeats lived here from 1880 to 1883. In more recent times the house was owned by Philomena Lynott, the mother of rockstar Phil Lynott, founding member of Thin Lizzy.

Continue through a car park to reach the Cliff Stop, a tea and ice-cream shop (it is closed during winter months). A gravel path flanked by bracken leads uphill at an information board at the rear of the car park. Climb the rocky steps to reach the clifftop above Puck's Rocks, a popular spot for sea angling.

After the first set of steps, leave the main trail and veer left along a smaller clifftop path for the best views. Meander along the path which is coloured by pink heather and coconut-scented yellow gorse. The path gradually rises to meet the main trail once again.

Concrete and wooden benches are placed at intervals along the clifftop trail. Throughout its stretch, the ground falls precipitously to the sea to the left. The sea cliffs here are an important summer nesting ground for guillemots, fulmars, kittiwakes and razorbills.

Another flight of steps leads to a flat area before the trail swings around to reveal the Baily Lighthouse, situated at the end of a long promontory in the distance. The lighthouse, built in the mid-seventeenth century, was finally completed in 1814. It was the last of Ireland's lighthouses to become automated.

The clifftop path undulates above Casana Rock, Piper's Gut and Fox Hole, then gradually rises to an area below The Summit car park. On reaching a marker post with multicoloured arrows, follow green, blue and red arrows pointing right. Climb the rocky steps, ignoring all subsidiary paths, towards a car park.

The Baily Lighthouse seen from the clifftop footpath below The Summit.

Just before reaching the car park, veer right to follow the green arrows (note: ignore the blue and red arrows pointing ahead). Follow a broad, distinct and sandy path, which is stony in places, to reach a T-junction. Turn left at the T-junction by a wooden gate and fence.

The path broadens and runs along the top of a low-lying ridge, giving views of Ireland's Eye and Lambay Island out to sea. At a cross-junction in the footpath, continue ahead. The path soon meets and descends Upper Cliff Road through a housing estate.

On reaching a T-junction with a bus stop in front, turn left along Thormanby Road, then right almost immediately into Dungriffin Road. After a bend, pass Thormanby Lawns estate on the right. Shortly after, turn right and go through a gap in a stone wall by a black rubbish bin.

Green arrows are signposted along a narrow, distinct and sandy laneway flanked by grass, bushes and trees. Howth Harbour and Ireland's Eye can soon be spotted ahead in the distance, a good indication you are heading the right way!

Continue along the laneway until meeting a road. Cross the road into a housing estate. Once in the housing estate, veer left almost immediately, keeping a concrete wall to your right. There are arrow markers on the wall. Follow the wall to its end and descend concrete steps flanked by metal railings.

At the bottom of the steps, turn left along a tarmac road. After a few metres and just before a bend leave the road and veer left onto a

Coloured trail markers along the clifftop footpath at Howth.

tarmac footpath. The footpath is signposted by coloured arrows on a lamp post.

The footpath is flanked by some trees on the left and houses on the right. Slightly beyond a right-hand bend, go through a gap in a low stone wall. A coloured arrow on a tree near the wall points the way forward.

The footpath meanders along a housing estate to the right and then goes under the cover of trees. It follows a wall over a stretch, before descending a ramp to reach a bus stop on the R105.

Howth DART station is directly opposite the R105. Turn right to pass The Bloody Stream, a popular seafood bar, named after a battle between the Normans and Vikings on St Lawrence's Day (10 August) in 1177.

Continue along the road to pass Howth Market shortly where you will find an array of Irish craft shops, organic food stores and shops selling artisan coffees and delicious home-made ice cream – it is worth a stop, as the car park at the start of the walk is not far away at all.

Howth Southern Loop

Howth's finest circuit: a summit with spectacular views, a lighthouse and an impressively wild coastline with dramatic sea cliffs, lovely coves and bays – what more can you ask for?

Grade:	2
Distance:	7.5km (4¾ miles)
Ascent:	200m (656ft)
Time:	3–4 hours
Map:	OSi 1:50,000 Sheet 50 or OSi 1:15,000 *Official Dublin City* and *District Street Guide*

Start/finish: The Summit car park on Howth, on the eastern end of the peninsula. Howth can be approached by car along the R105 from the city centre/Clontarf. If coming via the M50, head along the R139 (formerly the N32/Malahide Road) and follow signs for Donaghmede, Baldoyle and Sutton. At Sutton crossroads, turn right if coming from Clontarf or head straight ahead if approaching from Baldoyle. Follow the R105 along Greenfield and Carrickbrack Roads around the southern end of Howth for around 5.3km. When the road reaches the top of a rise, leave the R105 and turn right onto Thormanby Road. After around 100m, turn left at the Summit Inn to ascend Baily Green Road to reach The Summit car park at **O 295**₅₀ **374**₅₀.

The upper reaches of the Howth peninsula are predominantly quartzite. The rock, known locally as Howth Stone, is quarried and used in local buildings, stone walls and was also used in the construction of Howth Harbour. In this route, we will visit the highest point on Howth. Despite its mere height of 171m/561ft, the Ben of Howth gives spectacular 360º views of the surrounding area. From here, the trail leads southwards to a clifftop overlooking the sea. The coastline here along the southern end of Howth is surprisingly wild. A fine coastal path passes dramatic sea cliffs, a rocky foreshore, sheltered beaches, a secluded cove and the lovely Doldrum Bay. Save this route for a sunny day as the sea views along this southern end of Howth are stupendous!

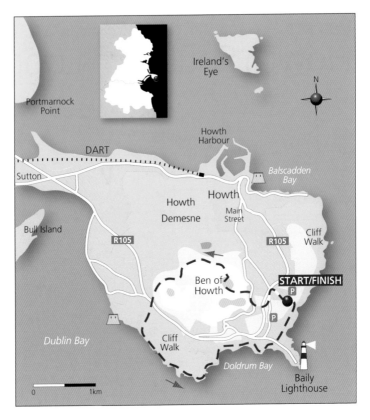

Route Description

Exit the car park under the height restriction barrier. Descend Baily Green Road to reach a junction of roads at the Summit Inn pub. There is a Red Trail arrow to the right of a postbox mounted in the wall ahead. Go left at the junction onto Thormanby Road and follow the Red Trail.

Pass the Summit Stores on the right. After another 100m, leave the road and turn right along a narrow earthen path flanked by bushes and trees. A Red Trail signpost points the way but this is easily missed as it is hidden by foliage.

Follow the path to meet Carrickbrack Road. Cross the normally busy road with care to meet a narrow path on its opposite end. A Red Trail marker is mounted on the lamp post showing the way. The earthen path is rocky in places and runs beneath a canopy of trees. It steadily rises to meet Woodgate Road above.

Looking northwards along the Portmarnock, Malahide and Donabate coastline from the Ben of Howth.

Turn right at Woodgate Road to pass some large walled and gated properties. After around 200m, veer left at a Red Trail signpost and go through a gap in the wall. An earthen path initially runs under the cover of trees. Once out of the trees, the path becomes stony and is flanked by bracken, gorse and heather. Some masts appear on the hillside ahead. When the path forks, veer left, still following the Red Trail signposts.

A distinct, firm path leads uphill to reach a junction on the right. Leave the Red Trail here and veer right onto a subsidiary path leading up towards a mast. When the stony and rocky path meets a broad track above, turn right and continue to meet the mast and trig pillar on the summit of the Ben of Howth at **O 285**₄₇ **376**₁₆.

The view is impressive and extends from the Wicklow Mountains in the distant south to the Portmarnock/ Malahide coastline in the north. North Bull Island is also prominent to the west and so too are the Poolbeg chimneys beyond. Closer still to the north, Howth Harbour can be seen, as well as the islands of Ireland's Eye and Lambay.

Retrace steps down the summit back to the Red Trail. Turn right there to shortly reach a junction of paths. Take the rightmost one, still following the Red Trail, and with all masts behind you.

Arrive at crossroads and turn right there. Now the Ben of Howth, its mast and trig pillar rise away to the right.

Right-of-way signposts and white stones guide the way through the golf course.

Clifftop footpath and concrete steps towards Drumleck Point along the Howth Head Loop.

On reaching a fork, take the left one and walk gradually uphill to meet a tarmac road. Veer left there onto the road.

Ignore an immediate junction to the left and keep following Red Trail arrows as the road bends to the right. Shortly after the bend, the tarmac ends and the road forks. Take the left fork (there is a Red Trail arrow on a rock there) and follow a broad dirt track beyond some boulders.

The track leads to a shoulder giving fine views of the Portmarnock/ Malahide coastline. Ignore all indistinct subsidiary paths and descend to a T-junction where there is a Red/Purple Trail signpost at **O 284**82 **379**59.

Turn left there onto a narrow path flanked by gorse and heather. The ground rises to your left as you meander along the path. Take a right at a fork to follow a Purple Trail signpost. As you descend along this path, Ireland's Eye and Lambay Island can be seen in the distance to your right.

Ignore all subsidiary paths and follow the main trail as it enters a shaded area. A rocky crag looms above vegetated slopes to the left. Two Purple Trail signposts appear in succession. Continue to the second signpost and bear left onto a short section of old railway sleepers.

The path leads to a golf course. Enter the golf course via a gap in the metal railings. Note the sign with the words 'PLEASE follow white stones and be alert to Golfers'. The white stones lead to a small white building. Keeping it to your left, follow green metal poles to a small earthen path nearby.

There is a similar 'Be alert to Golfers' sign here. Follow the firm path, which is flanked by tall bracken and gorse as it passes above the golf course. The course spreads out below and to your right with a backdrop of the coastline from North Bull Island to Portmarnock/Malahide.

The path descends to meet Carrickbrack Road. Cross the road and go through a gap in the wall near a metal railing. A stony path leads gradually downhill. The path turns grassy after some steps at a signpost. The sea can be soon seen ahead and also the twin chimneys of Poolbeg.

The path forks soon after passing between two stone pillars. Veer left here and continue along the grassy path to reach a T-junction. Turn right here and go through a gap between another two stone pillars.

The signposted path leads to a clifftop overlooking the sea. Go left and follow the clifftop path with the sea away to your right. Low-lying cliffs and crags loom ahead. The clifftop path soon leads to a flight of narrow steps carved in the rock.

Ascend the steps only to descend another series of steps back down onto the clifftop path. You will soon reach a fork at **O 272**₈₉ **367**₇₇. Ignore concrete steps leading uphill to the left, and take the right fork towards a rocky shoreline with a small sheltered beach.

The path next follows a stone wall and passes a white cottage. Steps have been put in place along the path in sections. At the end of the wall, and after passing a wooden fence on the left, arrive at a secluded cove near Drumleck Point at **O 277**₉₀ **363**₁₂. It is a good place to linger and take in the surroundings. Cormorants can often be seen perched atop one of the rocky pinnacles out to sea.

When ready, continue on the coastal footpath. A flight of steps runs by a fence, then the path swings round in an arc to reveal the Baily Lighthouse ahead. The lighthouse was moved to its current location in 1814 from somewhere near The Summit.

Ignore all subsidiary paths as the main coastal footpath passes above the lovely Doldrum Bay below sea cliffs to your right. The path soon runs along a private hedge decorated by exotic blooms along the landward side. Its seaward slopes are covered with bracken.

The path meanders under a shaded section of green shrubs and pine trees. After you pass a house perched precariously on the seaward side, the lighthouse comes into view again across a sea cove. Follow the path to reach a road.

If you wish you may turn right along this road and head south-east towards the lighthouse. This will add around 30–45 minutes to your journey. If not, cross the road to meet a track at a metal barrier.

The broad track soon dwindles to a narrow, firm, earthen and stony path. The path crosses the ravine of Whitewater Brook at a raised embankment. Pause here for one last look at the Baily Lighthouse away to your right. The path climbs a moderately steep slope to reach an area just below The Summit.

A multicoloured arrow points the way up to The Summit at the base of some steps carved out of rock. Veer left and ascend uphill to arrive back at the start.

St Anne's Park

A family treasure hunt awaits: to locate all the follies in the park! Other park attractions await too ... do I have to mention a playground and a rope swing?

Grade:	1
Distance:	2.5km (1½ miles)
Ascent:	30m
Time:	1–1½ hours but allow plenty more time for exploring the follies and othe distractions!
Map:	OSi 1:15,000 *Official Dublin City a District Street Guide*

Start/finish: Coming from Dublin city centre, go in the direction of Clontarf at the Alfie Byrne Road junction. Continue along Clontarf Road/ R807 for around 3.8km before turning left into Mount Prospect Avenue. After around 300m, turn right into the Red Stables car park. *By bus*: Dublin Bus No. 130 stops at Mount Prospect Avenue.

St Anne's Park was named by Sir Benjamin Lee Guinness in 1837 for a holy well located in its eastern end. The park contains a number of nineteenth-century follies, such as the Annie Lee Bridge, Herculanean House, Pompeian Temple and Roman Tower. However, many are currently in a serious state of neglect. The follies were constructed by Sir Benjamin Lee, son of Sir Arthur Guinness – the founder of Guinness stout and St James's Gate Brewery. Sir Benjamin was an antiquarian with a special interest in the monuments of Ancient Rome, which is evident from the design of follies throughout the park. Later, from 1875–1904, Lord and Lady Ardilaun continued to develop the park by introducing Main Avenue, the Naniken River trail, an ornamental pond and walled gardens. The Ardilauns also supervised the plantation of oak and other trees found in the park. This route traces a delightful path through the park, starting and ending at the Tudor-style Red Stables. It takes in all of the park's follies, along with its other attractions, such as Chestnut Walk, Naniken River, Main Avenue and Rose Garden.

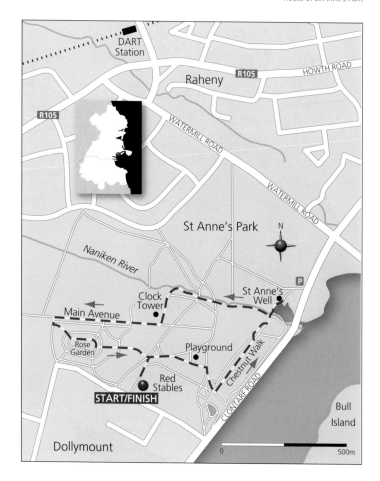

Route Description

Go through a gap between the red pillars on the left of the car park. Veer right onto the tarmac footpath with the Red Stables building, restored in 2006, to your right. A Farmers' Market, complete with amusement rides, takes place every Saturday (10 a.m. – 4 p.m. in winter, 10 a.m. – 5 p.m. otherwise) on an open area in front of the Red Stables.

Pass a carved wooden throne seat and a tree trail signboard to reach a neatly maintained grassy area of the park. Veer right at the signboard and continue to reach a playground. If not visiting it, keep the playground to your left and pass a spider-web climbing area and a rope swing to your right.

Chestnut Walk, St Anne's Park.

Turn right at a T-junction. The footpaths proliferate soon after. Take the leftmost footpath here to reach the Annie Lee Tower Bridge, or Sham Ruin. This folly was built to commemorate the birth of Sir Benjamin's first child, Annie Lee. Walk under the arch of the bridge, which was once the main entrance into the park and also driven under by Queen Victoria in 1900.

Soon after the Annie Lee Bridge, turn left into Chestnut Walk and stroll along its broad path under the cover of ash, horse chestnut and elm trees. There is a pond at the end of Chestnut Walk. Around 50m before the pond, climb some steps on the left of Chestnut Walk towards an embankment above. Reach a stone archway and continue along the top of the embankment towards the pond to reach a rustic bridge.

Veer left here into an area under the cover of trees to reach a circular, sunken basin surrounded by a circle of yew trees. Four marble Italian statues, representing the continents of Europe, Asia, Africa and America, once stood here by the marble basin and fountain. Slightly ahead of the Yew Circle, children will keep themselves busy with the 'monkey puzzle' tree, distinguishable by its large trunk and many protruding branches.

From the 'monkey puzzle' tree and Yew Circle, retrace steps back to the pond. Descend an earthen slope – taking care not to slip on tree roots – back down to Chestnut Walk. Turn left and head towards the ornamental pond to find mallard ducks and waterhens.

A Pompeiian Temple, designed in a Classical Italian style and used as a teahouse in 1898, can also be found here. A Roman Tower, obscured by trees, is also perched on top of a steep embankment to your left. The tower

Sunken basin and Yew Circle, St Anne's Park.

is based on the design of the Mausoleum of the Julii, one of the historic monuments of the ancient town of Glanum (*c.* 30 BC), and preserved today in St Rémy-de-Provence, France. The tower was originally located on top of the now demolished main house of the park, but Lord and Lady Ardilaun moved it to this location in the late nineteenth century.

It is possible to detour along a path on the left to the top of the embankment if you choose to visit the Roman Tower. If not, with the pond on your right, continue along its edge. Veer left just after it to find St Anne's Well sheltered by some trees. There is no altar at the holy well, but its water was said to provide virtues to pilgrims. Although the well is dry now, and has been for many years, an account from 1884 describes it as a 'natural spring'.

'Monkey puzzle' tree, St Anne's Park.

63

Roman Tower, St Anne's Park.

Retrace steps back to the start of the pond and veer right along a tarmac footpath sheltered by trees. The path runs along the Naniken River to its left. A few metres away, cross a bridge on your left to reach a rustic cave (which was constructed by the Ardilauns).

Retrace steps across the bridge then turn left to return to the path. After crossing another bridge, you will pass under a Herculanean House perched atop a steep embankment. An account by William Heale in 1873 describes it as 'built after a design of one at Herculaneum; from the stained glass windows there is a view of a romantic glen'. Herculaneum was an Ancient Roman town located in the shadow of Mount Vesuvius and was destroyed in AD 79 when the volcano erupted.

The footpath meanders in a semi-woodland area with the Naniken River now to your right. Squirrels, rabbits, hedgehogs and sometimes even foxes can occasionally be spotted among the trees. Ignore a bridge to your right at a crossroads. There are some stepping stones across the river a few metres after the bridge. Hop along the stepping stones here if you wish.

If not, continue along the main path to pass under a bridge which contains a Gothic-style hermit's cell. A remote-control car track and a dog park sit on a rise on the opposite bank of the Naniken River away to your right. Slightly further along the path is a low rustic bridge, under which adults will have to stoop in order to pass beneath.

Herculanean House, St Anne's Park.

Reach the Clock Tower on the right just after the bridge. The tower, the upper section of which is covered in ivy, was built in 1850 and has a clock with gold-leaf Roman numerals and skeleton hands. Turn right after the Clock Tower and walk along the wide tarmac footpath of the Main Avenue.

The Main Avenue is a mile (1.6km) long, but it is not our objective to walk the entire length of it. The tall, mature trees that flank the avenue are a mix of Holm oak and Monterey pine. Most of the trees were planted by Lord and Lady Ardilaun. Keep a lookout for red squirrels scurrying on tree branches as you walk by.

Clock Tower, St Anne's Park.

There is an entrance into the Walled Garden around 50m along Main Avenue. Take a detour if you wish to visit its herbaceous garden, plant nursery and fruit garden. If not, continue along Main Avenue until just before reaching some sports pitches away to your left.

Go left and follow signs here for the Rose Garden, which is divided into an inner and outer circle. The roses fully bloom in the summer, and you may wish to allocate some time to admire them in season.

The Red Stables building can be clearly seen from the Rose Garden. In your own time return to the car park at the Red Stables, or plan a visit to Olive's Room or Tir na nÓg Caife there.

North Bull Island Loop

Grade:	1
Distance:	6.75km (4¼ miles)
Ascent:	Negligible
Time:	2½–3½ hours
Map:	OSi 1:50,000 Sheet 50 or OSi 1:15,00 *Official Dublin City* and *District Street Guide*

A delightfully easy walk along a long, sandy beach and on the edge of salt marshes where birdlife is vibrant.

Start/finish: Coming from Dublin city centre, go in the direction of Clontarf at the Alfie Byrne Road junction. Continue along Clontarf Road/R807 for around 4.7km before turning right into Causeway Road. Continue along Causeway Road for around a kilometre before parking on either side of the road before the last roundabout, not far from the entrance to St Anne's Golf Club. *By bus:* Dublin Bus No. 130 – ask the driver to drop you off at the stop closest to North Bull Island/Dollymount Strand.

For centuries, the mouth of the River Liffey was blocked by silt and sandbanks, making it difficult for ships to navigate into and out of Dublin Port. The construction of the Great South Wall (5.6km) in 1795 and the North Bull Wall (2.75km) in 1824 created tidal currents which deepened the mouth of the Liffey by around 3m. Silt and sand were deposited over time on the North Bull, gradually forming an island. North Bull Island today extends north-east for around 5.6km from Bull Wall in the south to Sutton Strand at its tip. The sandy beach of Dollymount Strand runs along its entire south-east end, by the waters of Dublin Bay. The stretch of beach is backed by dunes anchored by sand sedge and marram grass. On the side of North Bull Island closer to the mainland is an extensive salt marsh backed by mudflats, visible only at low tide. The island has been designated as a UNESCO biosphere reserve since 1981, the only one located within a capital city in the world.

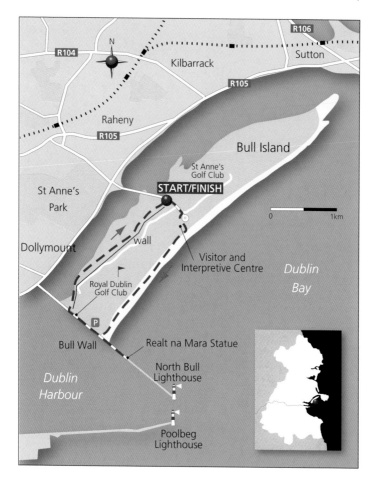

Route Description

Walk towards the roundabout to pass the Visitor and Interpretive Centre on your right. Continue ahead towards Dollymount Strand beyond a wooden barrier with a 'No Parking' sign and two large boulders. There are wooden picnic tables and benches here if you wish to have lunch with the family before setting off on the walk.

When ready, follow the road towards the beach to reach an area enclosed with large rocks, with a row of wooden posts and information boards away to your right. The expanse of beach is uplifting in contrast to the urban sprawl of the city. The Howth Peninsula provides the backdrop to the north-east.

The Dublin Mountains and the Poolbeg chimneys from Dollymount Strand.

Turn right and walk along the sandy beach. Look out for incoming or outgoing passenger ferries, such as Stena Line. The view ahead stretches from the south Dublin coastline to its docklands and twin chimneys at Poolbeg. The Great Sugar Loaf and part of the Wicklow Mountains, Killiney Hill and the Dublin Mountains form the hilly backdrop behind the city.

It is a pleasant stroll along the beach on the hard sand at low tide. When the tide is high, enjoy the spectacle of breaking waves. Gulls commonly flock here all year round. Keep an eye for sanderlings in the winter. These are small, pale wading birds whose black legs blur as they run back and forth on the sand.

Continue along Dollymount Strand to reach North Bull Wall after passing an area enclosed by large boulders, used as a public car park. A sandy slope leads to the top of Bull Wall. Turn left at the top of the wall and follow a tarmac footpath.

Pass two bathing shelters before reaching the *Realt na Mara* (Star of the Sea) Virgin Mary statue at the end of the wall. The statue, erected in 1972, stands on a tall tripod. There are benches in place and from here the views both seaward and inland are good.

Cyclist on Dollymount Strand with Howth in the background.

68

The Realt na Mara *(Star of the Sea) statue at the end of the Bull Wall.*

Retrace steps from the statue back inland along North Bull Wall. Reach the point at which you accessed the wall earlier and continue ahead to pass a car park (which has public toilets), a stone shelter and the Royal Dublin Golf Club. After the golf club reach a building used by the 5th Port Dollymount Sea Scouts.

Turn right at the building and go to its far end to meet an informal, grassy path that runs by a concrete wall. The coastal suburb of Clontarf, where Brian Boru claimed victory against his Irish and Norse enemies in 1014, can be seen across mudflats to the left. Follow a path that runs along the wall to reach the corner of a fence. Keep the fence to your right and follow a path to the end of the wall. Walk across a stony section, then regain the narrow, grassy path soon after.

The path follows a fence on the right and can be muddy in sections, especially after a wet day. The fence is broken in places, leaving only standing pillars. Follow the path as it meanders along the edge of the salt marshes for just over 2km.

The salt marsh is a bird sanctuary, best experienced at half-tide. It is filled with gulls, ducks and many other birds, such as redshank, curlew, oystercatcher, grey plover, dunlin and the seasonal brent goose.

Glasswort, with its fleshy scale-like leaves and autumn russet colour, can be found widely in the salt marsh. Thrift, with its pale pink flowers, is also common in the summer.

The path finally meets a grassy ramp that links back to Causeway Road. Emerge not far from the entrance to St Anne's Golf Club along the road. Turn right or left there depending on where your car is parked.

The view along the Bull Wall towards Clontarf.

Irishtown Nature Park and Poolbeg Lighthouse

Grade:	1 (Nature Park only); 2 (Lightouse extension, due to its length)
Distance:	3km (1¾ miles) Nature Park only, 10km (6¼ miles) Lighthouse extension
Ascent:	Negligible
Time:	1–1½ hours Nature Park only, 3½–4½ hours Lighthouse extension
Map:	OSi 1:15,000 *Official Dublin City* and *District Street Guide*

Start/finish: Park somewhere along Marine Drive in Sandymount (pay and display from 7 a.m. – 7 p.m., Monday to Saturday). If there are no spaces left, you may park at the top of Strand Road, near the south-east end of Sean Moore Park where it meets Beach Road. There may be some spaces also along Dromard Terrace, a side street off Marine Drive. Marine Drive may be approached by car via Merrion, Donnybrook, Ballsbridge or Ringsend – it is best to consult the *Dublin City and District Street Guide* for detailed road maps. *By bus*: Dublin Bus No.1 – ask driver to drop you off at the stop closest to Marine Drive. *By DART*: Exit at Lansdowne Road or Sandymount Station and walk towards Marine Drive using the *Dublin City and District Street Guide* road map.

Irishtown Nature Park is a small nature reserve on the southern end of the Poolbeg peninsula. The area of the park was once a dump in the 1970s for unused material and rubble from nearby construction sites during a building boom. The area was developed into a park in the 1980s following a meeting between the Sandymount and Merrion Residents Association and the then Dublin Corporation. Grass and trees were planted, as well as urban species like the buddleia. There are also some non-native plants, such as the hare's tail grass, with its distinctive, fluffy seed head, to be found. A collection of fungi, such as puffballs and chanterelles, also grow in the park. Irishtown Nature Park may be approached from Marine Drive at the south-east end of Sean Moore Park, or from the east end of the Poolbeg peninsula at the Shelly Banks car park. If approaching from Marine Drive, the route may be extended to take in the iconic red Poolbeg Lighthouse along the South Bull Wall (or Great South Wall), which adds 7km (nearly

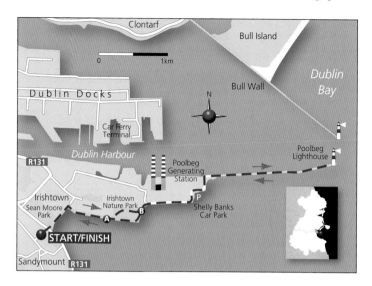

On the coastal fringes at Irishtown Nature Park with Shelly Banks beach and the Poolbeg chimneys ahead.

4.4 miles) to the length of the walk. A shorter there-and-back alternative approach to the lighthouse from the Shelly Banks car park is also provided. Whichever way you decide to approach the lighthouse, be well prepared

71

with warm and waterproof clothing, especially on windy and wet days, as the South Bull Wall is exposed except for some shelter at buildings just over the halfway mark. Note also that waves may break along the wall due to tidal conditions and ships' wash. While walking along the 2km stretch of wall to the lighthouse (and back!) keep a lookout for the common and grey seal, harbour porpoise, bottle-nose dolphin and minke whale, which can sometimes be spotted out to sea.

Route Description

Head towards the coast from Marine Drive and cross the road where Strand Road meets Beach Road, at the south-east end of Sean Moore Park.

Take the tarmac footpath that runs along the coastline, keeping the park and GAA grounds to your left. After around 400m, the footpath swings right, still following the coastline. The view of south Dublin Bay is expansive, with the Dublin Mountains rising as a sweeping mass in the distance.

As you continue along the footpath, take time to look behind to see the Aviva Stadium, rising above the River Dodder, around a kilometre away. Built on the site of the former Lansdowne Road stadium, the Aviva was officially opened in May 2010. Today, it is the home of the national soccer and rugby teams, as well as being a concert venue.

There are benches in places along the footpath if you need a rest. Around 650m after the bend, reach an information board for the Irishtown Nature Park (Grid ref: **O 199**11 **332**12) at Point A.

As you walk through the park, keep a lookout for birds such as the dunnock, greenfinch, goldfinch, skylark, wren, linnet, robin, stonechat and pied wagtail.

The tarmac footpath ends shortly after the information board and reaches a three-way junction. There is a narrow path to the right, and two broader paths to the left. Ignore the leftmost path running uphill and take the broad middle one. The path soon levels after a gentle rise before reaching a bend.

As you veer left at the bend, the beach at Shelly Banks comes into view. The beach is a popular spot for windsurfers, even in the winter. The twin chimneys of Poolbeg can also be seen towering ahead.

Around 200m after the bend, you will pass an earthen path on the left (Grid

Signboard for Irishtown Nature Park at Pigeon House Road.

ref: **O 203**33 **332**86) at Point B. If you wish to visit the Nature Park only, turn left here onto a path between the trees and continue along an earthen and grassy path.

Reach a fork after around 100m, and take a right here. A hum of machinery can be heard as the path passes close to the new incinerator, which is away to your right. Continue for a further 100m to reach another fork. This time take the left fork and follow the path as it descends to meet Point A again. From here, keep Dublin Bay to your left and retrace steps back to Marine Drive.

However, if you wish to continue to the Poolbeg Lighthouse from Point B, then continue along the coastal path and pass the Ringsend Wastewater Treatment Plant to your left. You will have to hold your breath as you pass the plant on windy days, and tolerate the foul smell coming from it.

There is an area of grassland near the Treatment Plant, which is provided and managed by Dublin City Council as a feeding area for brent geese. The geese winter here from December to March, flying as far as nearly 8,000km from Arctic Canada.

The path skirts around a sandy beach at Shelly Banks to reach Pigeon House Road, where there is a large wooden signpost for the Irishtown Nature Park. Here, turn right along the road, using either the footpath guarded by metal bars to the left; or a narrow, informal sandy path to the right.

Approaching Poolbeg Lighthouse, with Howth in the distance across the sea.

Walking away from the lighthouse with Poolbeg chimneys towering ahead and Dublin Port to its right.

The sheltered beach at Shelly Banks consists of sand dunes and marram grass, which is of conservation importantance. A variety of birds such as the black-headed gull, curlew, sanderling, turnstone and oystercatcher may also be spotted here.

The view across Dublin Bay to the right is extensive, with Killiney Hill a prominent landmark along the coastline, and the conical profiles of the Little Sugar Loaf and Great Sugarloaf in the background.

The road also runs along the Poolbeg Generating Station to the left, with the twin chimneys of the old Poolbeg Electric Supply Board (ESB) Generating Station standing guard, with their iconic red-and-white paint slowly fading away.

The car park at Shelly Banks, an alternative starting point for the route, is soon reached after a bend. At this point, the Poolbeg Lighthouse, a remote red landmark at the end of the South Bull Wall, comes into view.

For here, simply follow the coast road to reach a cul-de-sac, then veer right to walk the paved, uneven granite surface on top of the wall, which stretches for nearly 2km, to reach the lighthouse. Breakwater boulders are placed to the right of the wall, but some waves may still break over on windy days due to tidal conditions. This finger of granite walkway out to the lighthouse is exposed to the elements, except for the shelter at the Half Moon Swimming and Water Polo Club buildings just over the halfway mark, so ensure that children are well wrapped up in warm clothing and waterproofs.

As you approach the lighthouse, enjoy lingering vistas of the south Dublin coastline and the Great Sugar Loaf and Little Sugarloaf to the right;

of Clontarf and Dollymount Strand to the left; and of Howth ahead.

On the way back from the lighthouse, enjoy the views on both sides of the wall again, and now also of the twin Poolbeg chimneys and Dublin Port ahead.

If you need a cuppa, then look out for Mr Hobbs' coffee van at the start of the South Wall, which is there most weekends.

From here, simply retrace steps back to the Shelly Banks car park, or to Marine Drive, depending where you are parked.

Alternative start/finish point from Shelly Banks car park

The Shelly Banks car park may be approached by taking the turn-off for South Bank Road at the Sean Moore Road roundabout. Continue along South Bank Road for around 250m before taking the first left onto Whitebank Road. Continue along Pigeon House Road after a right bend. Pass the Dublin Bay Power Plant and continue along Pigeon House Road for just over 1km before taking two bends to reach the coastline. The road now runs along the coastline (with the Poolbeg Generating Station away to your left) for about another kilometre. Finally arrive at the Shelly Banks car park (Grid ref: **O 211**17 **335**00) after another bend in the road. From the Shelly Banks car park, you may choose to walk westwards and do a circuit of Irishtown Nature Park via Point B (there is no need to continue to Sean Moore Park but instead turn back at Point A), or head eastwards out to the Poolbeg lighthouse and back. Both are Grade 1 routes.

Distance: 3km (1¾ miles) Nature Park only, 5km (3 miles) Lighthouse only.

Time: 1–1½ hours Nature Park only, 1¾-2½ hours Lighthouse only.

Phoenix Park

	Grade:	1
Visit the best bits of Dublin's largest and most famous park on foot.	**Distance:**	7km (4¼ miles)
	Ascent:	Negligible
	Time:	2½–3½ hours but could be longer if you visit the playground and tearooms
	Map:	OSi 1:15,000 *Official Dublin City and District Street Guide*

Start/finish: Car park at the Phoenix Park Visitor Centre, signposted from the Phoenix Monument along Chesterfield Avenue. For directions how to get there see: www.phoenixpark.ie/visitorcentre/gettingthere/ The park is open all year round. Its main gates are at Parkgate Street and Castleknock Gate, which are open 24 hours a day. The park's side gates are open from 7 a.m. – 11 p.m. *By bus:* Dublin Bus No. 46A will stop at the Phoenix Park gates along Infirmary Road. Walk from the bus stop into the Park and along Chesterfield Avenue to the Wellington Monument. Walk the rest of the route clockwise from there. You may omit the Visitor Centre altogether at the Phoenix Monument roundabout and continue along the perimeter of Áras an Uachtaráin. After the People's Flower Gardens, head back onto Chesterfield Avenue. Turn left there toward the Phoenix Park gates and back to Infirmary Road.

The area around Phoenix Park dates back to 1177 when Hugh Tyrell, 1st Baron of Castleknock, granted land to the Knights of St John of Jerusalem at Kilmainham. These lands were seized by King Henry VIII in 1537. In 1662, a Royal Deer Park was established in the park grounds by Viceroy James Butler and included Kilmainham Priory demesne, south of the River Liffey. However, when the Royal Hospital was built in 1684, the park was reduced to its present size. Phoenix Park was opened to the public in 1747 by Lord Chesterfield and over a hundred years later, in 1860, it was placed under the management of the Commissioners of Public Works. In 1986, the park was designated as a National Historic Park. At 1,752 acres (707 hectares), it is one of the largest enclosed parks within a

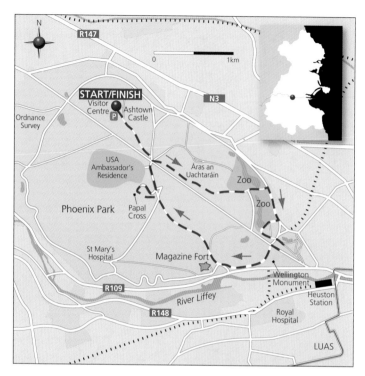

European capital city, and larger than all of London's parks put together. It boasts over 500 acres (200 hectares) of woodland consisting of ash, beech, horse chestnut, oak and sycamore trees. It also has 30km of footpaths, an 11km stone wall, 22km of roads, 14km of cycle lanes and a herd of around 450–600 fallow deer.

Route Description

Walk out from the car park of the Visitor Centre via its entrance. A tarmac footpath to the left of a metal fence leads towards a metal gate. The footpath meanders under the cover of trees to reach a network of roads at a roundabout. The Phoenix

Phoenix Monument.

Monument, erected by the 4th Earl of Chesterfield in 1747, sits in the centre of the roundabout. Its column is Corinthian in design with a phoenix rising from the ashes at the top.

Cross the road and pass the gates of Áras an Uachtaráin on the left, now the residence of the President of Ireland. It was the Viceregal residence from 1782–1922. The original two-storey brick house was built in 1751 by Nathaniel Clements for the Park Ranger and was purchased by the British Government in 1782. The house was transformed from 1802–49 to include the main ballroom, the stone south portico, formal gardens, dining room and drawing room (now An Grianán). In 1921, the first Governor General, Timothy Healy, took up residence, followed by other Governors until 1930. The house finally became Áras an Uachtaráin when Douglas Hyde became the first President of Ireland in 1938.

Go through a gap in a white metal fence and follow an informal, grassy path that runs along the green. The path runs parallel to the walled and fenced perimeter of Áras an Uachtaráin, around 50–100m away from Chesterfield Avenue. There are fine views towards the Dublin Mountains away to your right.

Follow the grassy path, keeping a spiked metal fence, black in colour, to your left. The path eventually meets a tarmac road. The Wellington Monument can be seen ahead in the distance, towering over the trees across the green parklands.

Follow a 3m-high meshed fence on the left bordering the Polo Grounds. Pass the Polo Building to your right and when the footpath forks, veer left, and walk between a set of metal poles. Pass the main gate of the Polo Grounds to your left and go through another set of white metal poles.

The footpath is now flanked by a stone wall and fence to your left and another 3m-high meshed fence to your right. The high fence to your right borders the grounds of Dublin Zoo. After around 100m, go through a gap of another set of white metal poles to reach a T-junction shortly after.

Turn right here and follow the footpath on the right of the road, with the high zoo fence to your right. Continue to reach a junction by the entrance of the Garda Headquarters. Turn right and pass the entrance of Dublin Zoo (resisting any temptation to enter, as a visit to the zoo is an all-day activity in itself!) to your right.

Soon after passing the zoo entrance, veer left through a gap in the black metal fence by a metal lamp post onto a tarmac footpath. Pass the Phoenix Park Tea Rooms to your left. The footpath leads down to a hollowed area under the shade of trees. A covered bandstand equipped with benches lies to your left.

The footpath rises to meet Fountain Road. Cross the road to enter the People's Flower Gardens through a metal gate at a fence. Walk towards an ornamental lake ahead and descend to a footpath by the water's edge.

Sean Heuston statue at the People's Gardens Park.

Wellington Monument in the Phoenix Park.

The footpath runs to the right of the lake. Continue to its end and descend some steps towards a playground. If not visiting the playground, swing around to follow the footpath that runs on the opposite end of the lake. Towards its end, veer left to reach the statue of Sean Heuston.

Keep the statue to your right and follow a footpath towards the Wellington Monument. It leads across the green and towards a gap in the metal fence in front of the George William Broderick (Chief Secretary of Ireland, 1835–1841) monument. Go through the gap and cross the busy road with care towards the Wellington Monument.

Turn right after crossing the road towards the roundabout. Turn left at the roundabout onto Wellington Road and go through a gap in the handrail on the left towards Wellington Testimonial.

This is an obelisk of around 62m in height, the tallest in Europe. It was built in 1861 to commemorate the victories of Arthur Wellesley, the Duke of Wellington. Four bronze plaques cast from cannons captured at Waterloo can be seen near its base – three have pictorial representations of the Duke's career while the fourth has an inscription:

Asia and Europe, Saved by Thee, Proclaim
Invincible in War Thy Deathless Name
Now Round Thy Frow The Civic Oak We Twine,
That Every Earthly Glory May Be Thine.

Magazine Fort in the Phoenix Park.

Retrace steps back out to Wellington Road and follow a footpath on the left of the road. Traffic sounds of the busy Conyngham Road fill the air and the Dublin Mountains fill the background view to the left. The footpath passes above the steps of the Conyngham Road pedestrian park entrance and the Royal Hospital Kilmainham, also to your left. There are benches on the roadsides if you need a break.

Descend to a crossroads after passing a large sports ground on your right. Turn right there to reach a car park at a lay-by on the left. Detour here by veering left and up the hillock to reach Magazine Fort. The fort was once used to store gunpowder and ammunition from 1735 through to the mid-twentieth century. It was occupied by the British Armed Forces up to 1922, then by the Irish Defence Forces after the Anglo-Irish Treaty. Having been demilitarised by the 1980s, the fort is now managed by the Office of Public Works.

Retrace steps back to the car park and veer left onto a broad tarmac footpath beyond some white metal poles. The footpath also has a cycle path and is a lovely, quiet section of the park. Keep a lookout for badgers, foxes, squirrels and rabbits here. The footpath rises gradually, giving a glimpse of the grounds of Áras an Uachtaráin away to your right. It then meanders under some tall pine trees to meet Acres Road. The Papal Cross can now be seen directly ahead.

Cross the road and head across a grassy area towards the 35m-high white Papal Cross, erected for the visit of Pope John Paul II on 29 September 1979. On this day, the Pope delivered an outdoor sermon to around 1.25 million people.

The cross overlooks the large green area of Fifteen Acres, where fallow deer graze, with the Dublin Mountains spread out in the distance. At its largest, the herd amounted to around 1,300 deer but this was reduced to only forty during the Second World War. Today there are around 450–600 deer in the parkland.

The Fifteen Acres may have once been the site of one of the earliest farming communities in Ireland. At its southern end near St Mary's Hospital, a burial cist was found under a mound of stones and soil. The cist contained urns of food vessels, baked clay, burnt bone and human skeleton dating to 3500 BC.

The Papal Cross on a grassy knoll near Fifteen Acres.

Retrace steps back out to Acres Road from the Papal Cross. Go left onto the footpath and pass the American Ambassador's Residence, built in 1774. Soon after, you will reach the Phoenix Roundabout again. Cross the road there and retrace steps back to the Phoenix Park Visitor Centre.

It is worth exploring the walled gardens, maze and demesne at the Visitor Centre. There is also a cafe and often exhibitions. Ashtown Castle, a seventeenth-century medieval tower house, also sits in the grounds of the Visitor Centre.

Ashtown Castle at the Visitor Centre, Phoenix Park.

81

Grand Canal and Dublin City Loop

Ramble along one of Dublin's best-known canals and visit some historic landmarks in the city centre.	**Grade:**	1
	Distance:	6km (3¾ miles)
	Ascent:	Negligible
	Time:	2–3 hours
	Map:	OSi 1:15,000 *Official Dublin City and District Street Guide*

Start/finish: Bord Gáis Energy Theatre in Dublin city centre. Park at Q Park, the Grand Canal Square underground parking off Chimney View near the theatre. For detailed directions how to get to the Bord Gáis Energy Theatre by car, bus (Dublin Bus No.15a/15b to Benson's Street along Sir John Rogerson's Quay), DART and LUAS see www.bordgaisenergytheatre. ie/getting-here

> *'Leafy-with-love banks and the green waters of the canal*
> *Pouring redemption for me'*
> **'Canal Bank Walk' by Patrick Kavanagh (1904–1967)**

The Grand Canal stretches westwards and is some 131km long. A total of forty-three locks are situated along its main line, which links Dublin to the River Shannon via Tullamore. The Grand Canal Way is a 117km-long National Waymarked Trail along the towpath from Lucan Bridge to Shannon Harbour. It is today managed, maintained and developed by Waterways Ireland, which also promotes over 1,000km of other inland navigable waterways in Ireland, such as the Royal Canal and Lower Bann. The idea of the Grand Canal was proposed as early as 1751 by the Commissioners of Inland Navigation, which consisted of public officials and private investors. Not long afterwards, the building of the canal started and then later, in the early nineteenth century, the Grand Canal became a thriving trade route whose cargo included turf and Guinness barrels. This paid activity was supervised by the Grand Canal Company and continued until 1950 before ownership transferred to Córas Iompair Éireann (CIÉ). Later, following the Canals Act 1986, the Grand Canal fell under the charge

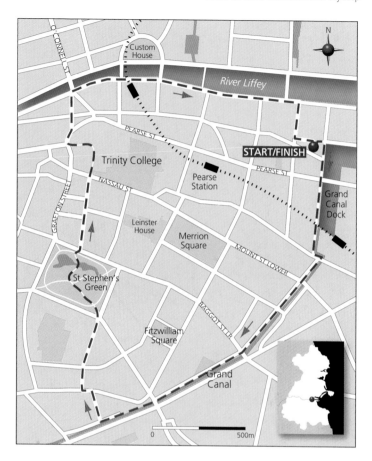

of the Office of Public Works. This route starts from the beginnings of the Grand Canal at the docklands and continues along the canal until just after Leeson Street Bridge. It swings back into Dublin city from there and charts a route back to the Grand Canal through some of Dublin's most popular spots such as St Stephen's Green, Trinity College and along the south quays of the River Liffey.

Route Description

At the Grand Canal Docks, with the Bord Gáis Energy Theatre away to your right, walk along Gallery Quay towards Pearse Street. Keep the canal to your left and pass some restaurants, a food market and delicatessen along Gallery Quay.

Cross Pearse Street at the traffic lights and continue ahead along Grand Canal Quay. Keep the Grand Canal to your left and pass the Waterways Ireland Visitor Centre (for details and opening hours see: www.waterwaysirelandvisitorcentre.org) on the left.

Walk on the pavement beside the cobblestoned street and pass The Malt House building on the left. Walk under the arch of a low bridge and continue to a T-junction. Turn left here, walk a few metres to the traffic lights and cross Grand Canal Street Lower.

Walk along the footpath with the canal to your left. Pass Locks C1 and C2 to reach Mount Street Lower. Cross the street at traffic lights to reach a bridge. On the left-hand side of the bridge is a plaque to honour the Irish volunteers who fought at the Battle of Mount Street Bridge during the 1916 Easter Rising.

Looking along the Grand Canal at Lock C1 towards Lower Mount Street.

Continue along the footpath with the canal on your left. Pass some ornate stone bridges near Lock C3, such as the 1791 Huband Bridge, named after Joseph Huband, a director of the Grand Canal Company.

Steps lead up to Herbert Place. Cross the road at traffic lights and continue under the cover of maple trees, with the canal still on the left. At Lock C4, there is a bench with a plaque dedicated to the Irish

Barges on the Grand Canal near Lock C4.

songwriter, artist and engineer Percy French (1854–1920) whose songs include 'The Mountains of Mourne'. Another bench on the opposite side of the canal is dedicated to the Irish poet and novelist Patrick Kavanagh (1904–1967) whose poems include 'On Raglan Road'. Use the wooden platform to cross the lock should you wish to visit it. If not, continue along the canal to reach a statue of Patrick Kavanagh sitting on a bench.

The following section of the canal is filled with reeds. Ducks paddle in the water and there are colourful recreational boats moored. Cross the road at Leeson Street Bridge at traffic lights. Continue along the section of the canal to the end of metal railings. The walls of houses to the right are coloured with graffiti. Before the pathway goes under the Luas line, leave the canal and turn right onto Harcourt Terrace.

Continue to a T-junction and turn left at Adelaide Road. Cross the road at the Presbyterian church onto Earlsfort Terrace. Pass the National Concert Hall and Conrad Dublin hotel to reach a crossroads opposite the entrance to St Stephen's Green.

St Stephen's Green was once marshy common land used for grazing livestock. The park was named after a thirteenth-century church nearby. In 1663, the City Assembly allocated 27 acres and built a wall that defined the park boundary. With the opening of Grafton Street (1708) and Dawson Street (1723), the Green became a valued location.

However, by the nineteenth century, the park's condition had deteriorated. Control was handed to local commissioners for maintenance and as a result it became a private park. Thankfully, Sir Arthur Guinness offered to buy the park in 1877, paid off its debts, redeveloped it and returned St Stephen's Green to the public. The park finally reopened its gates in July 1880.

Enter the Green via the large metal gates to meet The Three Fates sculpture, erected for the help given to German children after the Second World War. Take the inner footpath to the left of the statue. When the footpath forks at a water fountain, veer right and continue to reach landscaped gardens and fountain in a central area of the park.

Walk towards an ornamental pond and cross it via a stone bridge. Veer right immediately afterwards to exit the park via a small gate

The Three Fates statue, St Stephen's Green.

85

View of the lake at St Stephen's Green looking towards the ornamental gazebo.

onto St Stephen's Green Road. Turn left and cross the road onto Dawson Street. Pass the Mansion House, Cafe en Seine, St Ann's Church, Hodges Figgis bookshop and Lemon Crepe & Co. (worth a stop!) to reach the end of Dawson Street.

Cross the road here at Nassau Street and enter the Arts Block buildings of Trinity College – Ireland's oldest university founded by Queen Elizabeth I in 1592. Trinity graduates include writer Oliver Goldsmith, playwright Oscar Wilde and politician Edmund Burke.

Exit the building into Fellows' Square, following signs for the Book of Kells. The Book of Kells is an eighth-century manuscript of the four Gospels, which is decorated abstractly and artistically. Its exhibition is worth a visit (www.tcd.ie/visitors/book-of-kells). When ready, walk along a cobbled square, aiming for a gap to the left of the Book of Kells building. This leads into Parliament Square with Trinity's iconic Campanile (bell tower) and statues of historian William Lecky and mathematician George Salmon.

Go left in the square to pass between Trinity College Chapel and the Examination Hall and exit via Front Arch. Swing right here at College Green to pass the windowless, pillared Bank of Ireland building across the road on the left. Built in 1729, the building once housed the Irish Parliament. Continue ahead onto Westmoreland Street, passing the Westin Dublin hotel on your right.

Reach O'Connell Street Bridge, which spans the River Liffey. Built in 1790, it was originally named Carlisle Bridge, before being named after

Daniel O'Connell, 'the Liberator', in 1882. The Millennium Spire towers ahead. Do not cross the bridge but turn right onto Burgh Quay. Keep the River Liffey to your left and walk along the footpath beside the quay. Pass the Garda National Immigration Bureau and then the Immaculate Heart of Mary church to your right.

The 1791 Custom House, crowned by its dome and a statue representing Commerce at its top, and the International Finances Service Centre (IFSC) are on the opposite side of the river. Continue along the quay with the river still to your left to pass the elegant, cable-stayed Sean O'Casey Bridge. This pedestrian bridge is dedicated to the Irish playwright and chronicler of Dublin's working classes, Sean O'Casey (1880–1964) whose plays include *The Plough and the Stars*. A statue of an anchor in honour of seamen lost while serving on Irish merchant ships from 1939 to 1945 sits across the road there too.

Next, pass the Calatrava-designed Samuel Beckett Bridge, named after the Irish novelist, playwright and poet (1906–1989). This bridge was officially opened on 10 December 2009. Reach The Ferryman pub just after the bridge. Cross the road at traffic lights there onto Cardiff Lane. Continue along the lane, passing the Clayton Hotel to your right.

Just after the hotel, turn left onto Misery Hill beside the Bord Gáis Energy Theatre back to the start.

The view along the Liffey River toward the IFSC, the Sean O'Casey Bridge and the Samuel Beckett Bridge.

Dodder River Walk and Bushy Park

Go on a Native Tree Trail hunt in one of Dublin's suburban parks, visit its ornamental ponds and then walk along the beautiful Dodder River.	**Grade:**	1
	Distance:	3.75km (2¼ miles)
	Ascent:	Negligible
	Time:	1¼–2 hours
	Map:	OSi 1:15,000 *Official Dublin City and District Street Guide*

Start/finish: At the M50 Junction 11, take the N81 exit to Templeogue. Merge onto Tallaght Road (R137) and follow it for around 500m to reach a roundabout. At the roundabout, take the third exit. Continue for another 500m before turning left onto the R114. Follow it for around 1.4km, then turn left onto Fairways. Pass the Rathfarnham Shopping Centre on your left. Before reaching a T-junction, go left into the Tesco car park along the L8170. *By bus:* Dublin Bus No. 15b – ask to be dropped off at the stop closest to Rathfarnham Shopping Centre along Butterfield Avenue.

Around 1700, the Secretary to the Revenue Commissioners, Arthur Bushe, built a house known as 'Bushe's House' on a site of 11 acres (4.45 hectares) where Bushy Park sits today. It became known as Bushy Park in 1772 when its Dublin owner John Hobson named it after the Royal Park in London. Later, in 1791, the park was sold to Abraham Wilkinson who added another 100 acres (40.5 hectares) to the estate. Five years later, he presented the park as a dowry to his only daughter, Maria, on her marriage to Robert Shaw Jr. The Shaw family owned Bushy Park for 155 years before selling it to Dublin Corporation in 1951. In 1953, the Corporation sold nearly 20 acres (8 hectares) of the park to the Sisters of the Religious of Christian Education, including some woodland and pond areas. Nearly four decades later, in 1991, around 5 acres (2 hectares) of their grounds were sold back to the Corporation to be reintegrated into the park. Bushy Park has a Native Tree Trail, with fifteen trees to find by navigating your way around the park in this route. All trees have wooden marker signposts with more information. Native trees are species that have grown in their natural environment for thousands of years. In Ireland, this includes trees like the yew, common oak, birch and hawthorn. Besides the Native Tree Trail, this route also visits two ornamental ponds in the park before finally meandering along the picturesque Dodder River in suburban woodlands.

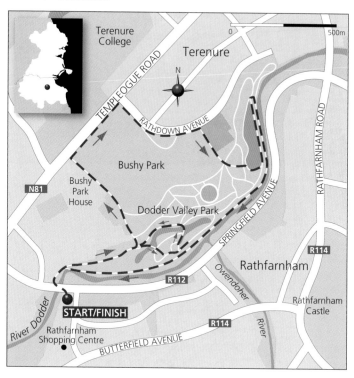

Bushy Park opens at 10 a.m. each day and closes at:
5 p.m. (December/January)
5.30 p.m. (February/November)
6.30 p.m. (March/October)
8.30 p.m. (April/September)
9.30 p.m. (May/August)
10 p.m. (June/July).
Note: park gates shut around half an hour prior to closing times.

Route Description

From the car park, head towards Springfield Avenue (R112). Cross the road at traffic lights at the T-junction of Fairways and Springfield Avenue. Turn

The Shell House with the bridge across the woodland pond in the background.

left and continue along Springfield Avenue to cross the bridge over the Dodder River.

Turn right after the bridge to descend some steps leading to a footpath below. The river now runs on your right. Leave the footpath shortly after and ascend some concrete steps by a stone wall.

Enter a swinging metal gate and follow a tarmac footpath beside a stone wall on your left. When the footpath forks a few metres ahead, veer left and meander under a canopy of trees. Keep a watchful eye for squirrels in the woodlands.

After the next junction, the tarmac footpath rises uphill to the left. Ignore that and continue ahead but shortly afterwards veer right to cross a bridge over a pond. There is a ruined building, known locally as the Shell House, on the left after the bridge. When the footpath splits into three, continue ahead leaving the bridge and ruined building behind.

A few metres ahead, the footpath reaches a Scots pine (*Pinus sylvestris*) with a wooden marker. Keep a wall to your right and continue along the footpath, ignoring all subsidiary paths. (Note that one of these subsidiary paths leads through the trees to a bridge away to the left.) Continue on the main footpath until reaching a holly tree *(Ilex aquifolium)* on the left.

Retrace steps back to the subsidiary path leading to a bridge noted earlier, veer right and head towards it. Cross the bridge over the pond. The kingfisher is often seen here so keep a lookout for it. Turn left after the bridge and continue along the footpath, with the pond now to your left.

Ignore the steps leading uphill on the right soon after, and continue along to reach a yew (*Taxus baccata*) and then an elder (*Sambucus nigra*). After the elder tree, the footpath arrives back at the first bridge across the pond.

Now veer right onto the tarmac footpath leading uphill. As the ground levels, ignore a footpath to the right. The footpath now follows the fenced boundary of an apartment block to your left.

A junction with sports pitches ahead is soon reached. Go left there keeping the sports pitches to your right and the apartments to the left. Some metal benches are installed along the footpath if you need a break. Along the footpath you will come across a young aspen (*Populus tremula*) and an apple tree (*Malus sylvestris*).

At the corner of the sports pitches, the footpath goes to the right. Follow this footpath, which runs along the busy Templeogue Road to the left. The footpath forks after an ash tree (*Fraxinus excelsior*).

Continue ahead to soon arrive at a hazel (*Corylus avellana*) tree. Soon after, reach the Rathdown Avenue entrance to the park. Walk away from the entrance and follow a footpath, keeping the sports pitches to your right. Stay close to the fringes of the park, with Rathdown Avenue now on your left.

Pass a common oak (*Quercus robur*) close to a sports building on the right. On the left of the building there is another wooden marker – a young bird cherry (*Prunus padus*) tree. You will have to leave the main footpath in order to view this young cherry tree.

Retrace steps back to the main footpath to reach the entrance of the park by some tennis courts. Follow an earthen path, keeping the tennis courts to your left and sports pitches to your right.

The path turns into tarmac again at the Sportsworld Running Club building. When the paths proliferate ahead, veer left to reach another wooden marker post and tree – the mountain ash (*Sorbus aucuparia*).

Retrace steps to the proliferation of paths earlier and now veer left to descend a tarmac

Duck pond at Bushy Park.

Dodder River.

footpath down to a bandstand. There is a large green area to the left and a playground nearby. Veer left across the grassy meadow towards the hawthorn (*Crataegus monogyna*). The meadow is an area of wildflower plants such as the oxeye daisy, field scabious, lesser knapweed and teasel, which all provide food and shelter for bees and butterflies.

A large ornamental pond with a central island of trees and shrubs can be seen nearby. The pond has a large number of wildfowl such as mallard, tufted duck, mute swan, coot, moorhen and little grebe. There is also a mix of aquatic and wetland plants around the pond such as the bulrush, common reed, flowering rush, marsh marigold and the yellow water lily.

Descend the ramp to the pond. Walk in a semicircle with the pond to your left and a stone wall to your right. Shortly after the footpath passes under the bandstand, veer right to find a young birch (*Betula pendula*) on a grassy embankment.

Later, retrace steps back to the pond. Keep it to your left and follow the footpath to pass a gated archway to your right. Sounds of traffic can be heard and there are wooden benches placed along the footpath.

Pass an alder (*Alnus glutinosa*) followed by a gap in the wall and continue to the end of the pond. Just beyond the pond is the final wooden marker and willow (*Salix species*).

Retrace steps from the willow back towards the pond and go through the gap in the wall. Keep the 3m-high wall to your right and walk along a footpath with the Dodder River now to your left.

Ignore a bridge over the river and continue along the footpath under the cover of trees to reach the steps at the start of the walk. Retrace steps from there back to the start.

Marlay Park

This popular south Dublin park has it all: beautiful woodlands, a duck pond, an idyllic stream, stone bridges, cafes, a golf course, a playground, a miniature railway, a walled garden and a Fairy Tree!

Grade:	1
Distance:	3km (2 miles)
Ascent:	Negligible
Time:	1–1½ hours but plenty of distractions to consume more time!
Map:	East West Mapping 1:30,000 *The Dublin Mountains & North Wicklow* or OSi 1:15,000 *Official Dublin City and District Street Guide*

Start/finish: Leave the M50 at Junction 13 and take the R826 exit for Sandyford/Dundrum. Take the first exit onto the R133 at the roundabout. After around 1.3km, turn left into Grange Road/R822, following signs for Ticknock. Arrive shortly at the Marlay Park entrance on the right. There are ample spaces at a car park there. *By bus*: Dublin Bus No. 16 – ask to be dropped off at a stop close to the park entrance along Grange Road.

Marlay Park sprawls across the foothills of the Dublin Mountains over an area of around 300 acres (121 hectares). The park is of an early nineteenth-century English landscape design, developed by gardeners Brown and Repton. The name Marlay comes from the daughter of the Bishop of Dromore, Elizabeth Marlay, who married Frenchman David La Touche. La Touche later purchased the Marlay estate from the Taylor family in 1764. The estate was finally purchased by Dublin County Council in 1972 and developed into a public park, which was opened in 1975. Today, the park also provides amenities such as playgrounds, a golf course, football and cricket fields, tennis courts, a model railway, a walled garden and craft centre. During the summer months, the park holds many concerts and events such as the Longitude Festival.

Marlay Park opening hours are:
9 a.m. – 5 p.m. (Nov/Jan)
9 a.m. – 6 p.m. (Feb/Mar/Oct)
9 a.m. – 8 p.m. (Sept)
9 a.m. – 9 p.m. (April)
9 a.m. – 10 p.m. (May–Aug).

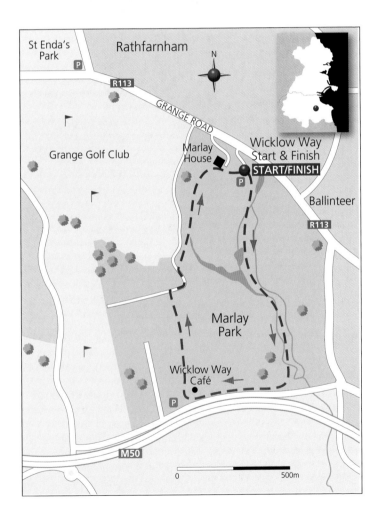

Start of the Wicklow Way at Marlay Park, with Marlay House in the background.

Route Description

Go to the information boards at the far end of the car park. There, a stone wall marks the start of the Wicklow Way just before a large expanse of green parklands. Marlay House, a restored Georgian house, is also away to your right.

The Wicklow Way is marked by Yellow Man signposts, your guide for the first half of the walk. Formally launched in 1981 by J. B. Malone, the Wicklow Way is the oldest long-distance waymarked trail in Ireland. Extending for some 127km from here to Clonegal in County Carlow, it is also part of the 4,700km European E8 walking trail which begins in Cork and ends in Istanbul, Turkey.

Footpath under the cover of trees at Marlay Park, just before the Fairy Tree.

Follow the tarmac footpath into the green area. The Yellow Man points ahead at a crossroads. Take the inner footpath straight ahead which meanders under the cover of trees (the outer one runs along the green – don't take that). The footpath follows close by a stream which can be heard on the left. At a junction with 'Tennis courts/Playground BMX' signs, continue ahead to follow the Yellow Man signs.

The path crosses a bridge and then reaches a three-way junction. Veer right here, still following Yellow Man signs and shortly afterwards pass a pond on the right. Children may wish to take a short detour to the viewing deck by the pond and watch the ducks.

Retrace steps when done and continue along the Wicklow Way, which now follows a stream on the right. Continue ahead at a fork, still following Yellow Man signs. The path soon crosses a stone bridge where a cascade flows down a rocky section.

Take a left immediately after the bridge at the crossroads. Continue through the woodlands before shortly arriving at the Fairy Tree with towers around the top, and a staircase, horseshoe-shaped windows and

The Fairy Tree in Marlay Park.

a little door at the base. Holly trees that grow in the vicinity give it a Christmassy feeling and the nearby stream makes for an idyllic setting.

Continue ahead at the next junction, still following Yellow Man signs. The path soon passes another stone bridge away on the left before reaching a T-junction. The Yellow Man sign points right there, with signs also for 'College Road/Playground'.

Turn right here onto the path that runs parallel to a large stone wall on the left. College Road and the M50 are beyond the stone wall, giving rise to the momentary noise of motor vehicles interrupting the tranquillity of the park.

Pass a set of outdoor fitness equipment before arriving at a large car park on the southern end of Marlay Park. The Wicklow Way Cafe here is an ideal stop for snacks and refreshments. A challenging nine-hole putting adventure golf course for the family can be found behind the building.

This is the point where you leave the Wicklow Way, which itself ascends into the foothills of the Dublin Mountains, so turn right before the car park. Keep the Wicklow Way Cafe and golf course away to your right, and continue ahead along the tarmac.

Midway down the footpath, you may wish to take a short detour to a large playground on the left. If not, continue ahead to pass some soccer pitches and tennis courts. Enter a gap through the wall to reach a T-junction. Before turning right onto a road there, you may choose to have a look at the Dublin Society of Model and Experimental Engineers (DSMEE) Miniature Railway just ahead (open Saturdays 2.30 p.m. – 5 p.m.).

The road is bordered by a stone wall and passes more soccer pitches on the right with a scenic backdrop of Three Rock Mountain and its masts in the distance. The road passes a maintenance building on the left. At a

Entering the walled garden at the back of Boland's Cafe in Marlay Park.

bend just after the building, there is a small gate on the right. Leave the road now and go through a gap in the wall there.

Continue ahead at a junction immediately afterwards to reach another junction with a Regency Garden sign pointing left. Continue ahead and cross one of two bridges across a stream into a large green area.

Turn left here and now walk along the footpath, keeping the green to your right. Follow the footpath back towards Marlay House, which is clearly visible ahead. Boland's Cafe before the House is a tempting stop for coffee and a cake or pastry. There is a Regency walled garden at the back of the cafe with an ornamental garden, bird aviary and a garden school which might be of interest to children. In your own time, leave the cafe behind and head towards Marlay House to arrive shortly back at the start.

Sandycove Heritage Trail

History and the sea await in this stroll around the fascinating seaside town of Sandycove.

Grade:	1
Distance:	3km (2 miles)
Ascent:	Negligible
Time:	1–1½ hours
Map:	OSi 1:15,000 Official *Dublin City and District Street Guide*

Start/finish: Leave the M50 at Junction 16 and take the R118 exit to Cherrywood/Loughlinstown. At the roundabout take the second exit onto Cherrywood Park/R118. Continue for around 3km to reach Graduate Roundabout. Take the second exit at the roundabout and stay on the R118. At Glenageary Roundabout, take the third exit onto Glenageary Road Lower/R118. Go through a small roundabout and follow the road to reach traffic lights with People's Park ahead. Turn right there onto Summerhill Road/R119 and continue for around 250m. Turn right into Eden Park just after Sandycove/Glasthule DART Station and park there.

The name Glasthule was derived from *Glas* ('a small stream') and *Tuathail* (Toole, a surname). The railway there was opened in 1855 by the Dublin and Kingstown Railway Company, forming part of the Dublin–Bray coastal line. Kingstown is the old Victorian name for Dún Laoghaire, following a visit by King George IV in 1821. The present name, Dún Laoghaire ('fort of Laoghaire'), was adopted again in 1920. A 2m-high sculpture made from Kilkenny limestone sits in Eden Park, where the walk begins. The sculpture, created by Dick Joynt, is called 'Celebration' and depicts a woman holding her child up in the air, celebrating life. The walk initially charts a course through the tidy streets of Sandycove, passing an old church, pubs, an old archway and historic buildings before veering seawards to Sandycove Beach. It takes a detour to visit the famous James Joyce Tower & Museum and Forty Foot bathing place, before a delightful stretch along the fringes of Scotsman's Bay.

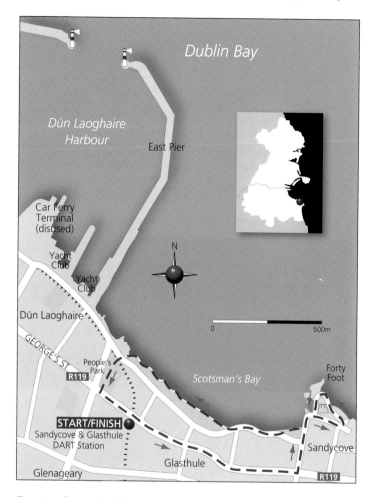

Route Description

Exit the car park and turn right onto Summerhill Road to join up with Glasthule Road at St Joseph's Church. The church, designed in neo-Gothic style by architects Pugin and Ashlin, was built in 1868.

Pass the church to reach traffic lights at Eagle House pub, adorned with distinctive arched windows. The building dates back to the early 1900s. Cross the road and pass Glasthule Gallery on the left, before the road is flanked by some houses.

Just after passing Wilmont Avenue, there is a plaque to commemorate the James Joyce Bloomsday Centenary. There are colourful celebrations

Looking across Scotsman's Bay toward Dún Laoghaire from Sandycove Beach.

here annually on 16 June. Next, pass Marine Avenue, followed by Burdett Avenue, to reach a junction with the Charles Fitzgerald Pub at the corner. The pub has a stained-glass window illustrating scenes from *Ulysses*.

At the corner of a row of shops on the left is Ballygihen Archway, built in 1840, with its weathervane perched atop. You are now on Sandycove Road and shortly you will pass Tara Hall on the right. Tara Hall was once the house of the author and poet Monk Gibbon (1948–1985) who did all

James Joyce Tower at Sandycove.

his writing in bed. The house has a plaque on the wall and is now a bed & breakfast. However, it was once a meeting place for Irish writers such as Austin Clarke and Padraic Colum.

A few blocks away is No. 29 Sandycove Road, where Sir Roger Casement, a leading figure in the 1916 Rebellion, is said to be have been born. On reaching a set of traffic lights, turn left into Sandycove Avenue West following signs for James Joyce Tower. Walk down the quiet side street, passing No. 26 on the left, former home of the portraitist Edward McGuire, famous for his oil-on-canvas representation of Seamus Heaney.

The seafront soon comes into view at a crossroads. The house on the right is Sandycove Castle, a fine example of a Victorian villa. Originally called Cove Castle, it was once a school for young ladies. Continue along to reach an enclosed toilet block on the left (50c to enter, at the time of writing – no change given!) and the Curragh Sub Aqua building.

At the horseshoe-shaped Sandycove Beach, there are fine views north-west towards Dún Laoghaire and north Dublin with the twin chimneys at Poolbeg. Follow the road that bends to the right at the beach. Ignore a junction on the left and continue along Sandycove Avenue North. Reach a three-way junction and turn left towards a cul-de-sac by the sea.

Take a left almost immediately and walk towards the James Joyce Tower, which is now visible ahead. This is a Martello tower built in 1804 during the Napoleonic Wars and occupied by the military until 1900. During his six-day stay here in September 1904, James Joyce wrote the first chapter of his literary classic *Ulysses* from the platform on the roof. The sea is now on your right as you approach the tower. There is a museum here, too, which houses rare first editions of Joyce's work and personal memorabilia, including letters and photographs.

The road then descends to reach a deep-water pool known as the Forty Foot away to your right. Originally called the Forty Foot Hole in the 1800s, the spot is named after the Fortieth Foot Regiment which was stationed at the battery above. This is a popular spot for an annual Christmas Day charity swim.

Follow the road as it swings back to Sandycove Beach. The small harbour here was built in 1735 and used to ship granite from Dalkey Quarry to Dublin. It was also the berth of Dún Laoghaire's first lifeboat in 1803. Partially retrace steps earlier and just after reaching an ornate green Irish Free State postbox in the wall, veer right into Sandycove Park and towards the promenade.

A few metres away on the right is the Peace Tree with a plaque at its base. The tree, a walnut sapling, was planted in 2007 to commemorate the restoration of a devolved government in Stormont in Northern Ireland. Continue along to pass an information board before reaching the Joyce Memorial Plaque by a tree on the right. The plaque was erected in 1982 to mark the centenary of Joyce's death.

Sculptures at Newtownsmith Park: (l–r) Archer II and Mothership.

Scotsman's Bay, named after John Rennie, the Scottish engineer who designed its harbour in 1859, is now on your right. The bay is a nursery ground for crustaceans and young fish, and also a habitat for seabirds such as the Arctic tern, common tern, cormorant, grey heron, oystercatcher and sandpiper.

Continue along the promenade through Newtownsmith Park, which was once a rocky foreshore. Views out to sea extend to North Bull Island and Howth. There is an outdoor fitness area in the park, and also benches to use if needed.

Pass the 1921 Marine Parade Monument, known locally as the 'horse trough', away on the left followed by the Archer II sculpture. The sculpture, which represents energy, is made from white concrete and steel. The archer's arrow is aimed out towards the James Joyce Tower.

Continue along the promenade to reach the Mothership, an ornate cast-bronze sculpture that looks like a giant sea urchin, with a central, circular opening. From here, continue to the end to a blue wall with the words painted in white: 'The first faint noise of gently moving water broke the silence, low & faint & whispering', a quote from Joyce's *A Portrait of the Artist as a Young Man*.

Leave Newtownsmith Park here and head towards Promenade Bistro and Teddy's Ice-cream Shop. Cross the road with care, turn right and continue on to reach the steps leading into People's Park.

People's Park, designed in 1890 by architect J. L. Robinson was reopened by Dún Laoghaire and Rathdown County Council on 21 May 2015. The park was a quarry in the late eighteenth century and granite quarried here was used to build Dún Laoghaire Harbour.

Veer left up the steps and enter the park. There is a playground away to the left. Pass some cast-iron Victorian fountains and head towards the Fallon & Byrne restaurant and coffee shop at the end of the park.

Exit through a gate to the left of Fallon & Byrne. Turn left on the road and continue to the traffic lights. Cross the road, turn left and head back to Eden Park at the start.

People's Park, Dun Laoghaire.

Dalkey Quarry, Dalkey Hill and Killiney Hill Circuit

Watch rock climbers in action, go on a folly hunt and enjoy far-reaching views of the Dublin and Wicklow coastlines from the upper reaches of Dalkey/Killiney.

Grade:	1
Distance:	2.5km (1½ miles)
Ascent:	100m (328ft)
Time:	1–1½ hours
Map:	OSi 1:15,000 Official Dublin City and District Street Guide

Start/finish: Leave the M50 at Junction 16 and take the R118 exit to Cherrywood/Loughlinstown. At the roundabout take the second exit onto Cherrywood Park/R118. Continue for around 3km to reach Graduate Roundabout and take the third exit onto Ballinclea Road. Shortly afterwards, at a fork, veer right to stay on Ballinclea Road. Continue for around 1km then turn right onto Killiney Road. Turn left at the T-junction onto Dalkey Avenue and go through a small roundabout. Ignore Ardburgh Road on the right and take the next sharp right onto Burton Road (or The Metals). Pass a large playground on the right and drive uphill to reach the car park at Killiney Hill Park.

This route takes in three main attractions accessible from the car park: Dalkey Quarry, Dalkey Hill and Killiney Hill. It also visits follies and the high point at 153m/502ft. Despite being in an urban area, Killiney Hill has a surprising population of mammals such as bats, foxes and red squirrels. There is also large variety of birds such as chiffchaffs and warblers that live in its mature woodlands of beech, sycamore, oak and pine trees. The area is also home to around 200 native and introduced plant species, including the burnet rose, sea spleenwort, golden samphire, rock samphire, bluebells and common ragwort. A local variety of hybridised ragwort called Dalkey ragwort is said to have originated from a garden at the nearby Sorrento Cottage. Although the bedrock of Dalkey Hill and Killiney Hill are composed of granite and mica schists, the lower slopes of both have a thick layer of calcareous drift. This and a mix of sea air provide a unique habitat for the many plant species to thrive here.

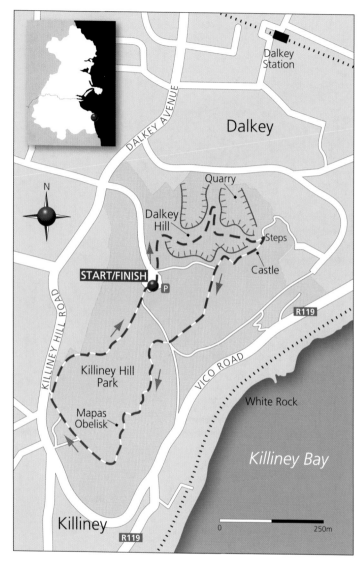

Route Description

There is a Dalkey Community Council plaque dated March 1995 at the entrance of the car park on the elevated area. Footpaths proliferate after the plaque. Ignore ones leading uphill and take the tarmac footpath to the left.

Flight of steps at the back of Dalkey Quarry leading to Dalkey Hill.

The playground is now below you to the left, with Dún Laoghaire town and harbour in the distance ahead. The town is named after a fifth-century Irish High King, Lóegaire mac Néill. In 1821, it was renamed Kingstown, in conjunction with King George IV's visit. However, it reverted back to its original name in 1920 in the lead-up to Irish independence.

The footpath soon swings right, with the sea now to the left in the distance. Pass a rubbish bin at the end of a stone wall and follow the footpath into Dalkey Quarry. The Metals Walkway, a small railway with iron tracks, used to run from Dalkey Quarry to the West Pier in Dún Laoghaire. Constructed in 1816, it was used to transport granite from the quarry for the construction of Dún Laoghaire Harbour.

Looking down on Dublin city from the wall on Dalkey Hill, with Three Rock Mountain to the distant left.

A flight of steps can be seen at the back of the quarry rising steeply to a gap in a stone wall above. As you walk along the main footpath, huge slabs rise on the right and lush valleys can be seen over the top of cliffs to the left.

Leave the main footpath and take a subsidiary path to the left, flanked by gorse. The path meanders along the top of cliffs, 30–40m high, with dizzying drops down into flat, sheltered green areas below. This area of the quarry is popular with rock climbers, and you might see some in action.

Be very careful along this section, especially with young

Descending the path by the ruined wall under pine trees.

children and do not go anywhere near the edge of cliffs. If you prefer to err on the side of caution, you may omit this section altogether. Retrace steps back to the main path when done.

Veer left along the main path and continue in the direction of the steps at the back of the quarry. Ascend the steps using the metal handrail on the left for support if needed. The steps climb steeply next to a rocky crag on the right.

At the top of the steps turn right. Follow a stone wall, ascend some more steps and go through a gap in the wall to reach Telegraph Tower on Dalkey Hill. The stone tower was built in 1807 as a signal station to several Martello towers along the east coast and used during Napoleonic times.

The views into Dalkey Quarry and across to Dún Laoghaire harbour and the sea are impressive from the wall by the tower. Go through another gap in the wall and now enjoy views on its opposite side towards the expanse of Killiney Bay with the Great Sugar Loaf and the distant Wicklow Mountains as its backdrop.

Stay on the main path to pass a radio beacon on the left, or you may choose to detour along a subsidiary path on the right which follows the wall and reveals fine vistas into the quarry, Dún Laoghaire and across the sea to Howth. When the wall takes a sharp turn right and starts to fall, veer left to rejoin the main path.

Back on the main path, descend until reaching a fork. Leave the main path here and veer left, following steps down onto a narrower path. This path runs by a ruined wall and meanders under pine trees near an area of woodlands. The Great Sugar Loaf and the sea are visible to the left beyond a rocky area splattered with gorse.

Further along, a set of concrete steps leads to a crossroads with stone pillars to the right and an information board on the left. Walk ahead through a gap in the wall and ascend another series of concrete steps to reach the Step Pyramid. Built in 1852, it is known locally as The Wishing Stone and will, according to local legend, grant your wish – walk around each level, then stand on top and make a wish!

The ground rises to reach the large, hollow cone of the Mapas Obelisk at the top of Killiney Hill. There is another smaller folly below steep, shrub-covered slopes to the east: the small cone of Boucher's Obelisk, known locally as the Witch's Hat.

Work on the Mapas Obelisk, built entirely of rubble granite, was commissioned by Colonel John Mapas and carried out by labourers during the famine winter of 1741. There are 360° views of the surrounding area from here, and on a fine day you might even see the Welsh mountains, almost 160km away across the Irish Sea!

Having enjoyed the views, keep the Mapas Obelisk on the right and descend Killiney Hill along a broad tarmac footpath. There are benches in place if you need a rest. The footpath leads steeply down to the Killiney Hill Road gated entrance.

There is a statue there called Daedalus Flew, named after the craftsman of Greek mythology, Daedalus. The master craftsman made the wings that he and his son Icarus used to flee from captivity in Crete.

The Tower Tearoom here offers snacks and refreshments. There are also public toilets should you need them.

If not, continue following the footpath as it undulates back to the car park at the start.

Looking across Sorrento Point to Dalkey Island from Killiney Hill. The folly below is the small cone known as Boucher's Obelisk.

Rathmichael Woods Circuit

An easy woodland walk on the foothills above Shankill to an elevated site giving commanding views of Bray Head and the Sugarloafs.

Grade:	1
Distance:	2km (1¼ miles)
Ascent:	50m (164ft)
Time:	1 hour
Map:	OSi 1:50,000 Sheet 50

Start/finish: The entrance into Rathmichael Woods along Puck's Castle Lane at **O 232**44 **213**03. This is best approached off Ballycorus Lane, along the R116 between Kilternan and Shankill. There are spaces for two to three cars near a signboard for Rathmichael Woods.

This circuit around Rathmichael Woods is a pleasant stroll through broadleaved and coniferous woodland. The wood is intermixed with acid grassland and scrub which provide an ideal habitat for birds, butterflies and bumblebees. Keep an eye out for mammal species such as the red fox (*Vulpes vulpes*) and pygmy shrew (*Sorex minutus*) in the cover of the woods. The pygmy shrew is Ireland's smallest mammal, weighing around 6g. Adult pygmy shrews have brown fur, lighter on the sides and underbelly, and a thick, hairy tail. The main attraction of this walk is a rath or hillfort, although all that remains today is just a grassy mound overlooking Rathmichael and Shankill. During its heyday, the site was probably the gathering place of a rich local chieftain and his clan.

Route Description

Follow the Yellow Man Dublin Mountains Way signs into the woods. A broad track descends to reach a pond where views of the Little Sugar Loaf and the sea appear in the distance.

The track bends left at the pond, then forks soon after. Take the right-hand fork and follow the Yellow Man signs or the Green Trail (denoted by a white arrow on a green background).

When the track forks again, ignore the branch going downhill and take the left-hand path. The track passes under birch and pine trees and is flanked by high gorse bushes and bracken.

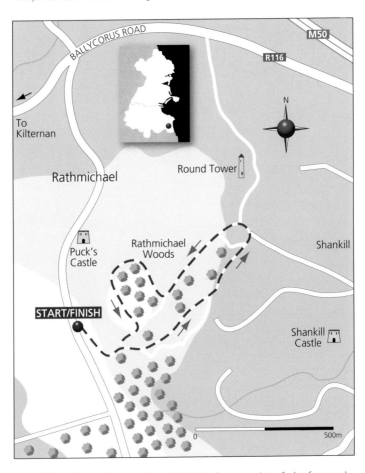

Follow the track to reach a wide circular area. At a fork afterwards, ignore the track leading uphill and take the right-hand fork. Soon after, ignore a junction to the left and continue ahead, still following Yellow Man and Green Trail signs.

On reaching a T-junction with an information board, the Yellow Man sign points along a lane to the right whereas the Green Trail points left. It is worth taking a short detour, by turning right and walking around 250m along this lane to reach the twelfth-century Fassaroe Cross boundary marker. This marks the entrance to an old church nearby. The short granite cross depicts the crucifixion scene on a wheel-shaped head with projecting arms.

If not taking the detour to the Fassaroe Cross, turn left at the T-junction and follow the Green Trail. The forest track gradually rises to meet a

On the forest track at Rathmichael Woods, with Dalkey Island in the distance and Killiney Hill hidden behind a tall hedge of gorse to the left.

junction on the left. Continue ahead there, still on the Green Trail, as the track rises again.

A tall hedge of gorse blocks the view onto a grassy field to the right. As height is gained, glance back the way you came for some fines views out to sea. Killiney Hill and its obelisk can also be seen in the distance, with Howth as its backdrop.

As the track rises further, a gap appears through the gorse and trees, revealing fine vistas out to the Little Sugar Loaf and Great Sugar Loaf to the south. When the track levels off, it reaches a junction to the right.

A signpost for the Green Trail points to the right here. Follow it on the dwindling track under the cover of tall pine trees. The path soon forks a few metres ahead. Turn right there

Pine tree at the hillfort site at Rathmichael.

111

Looking towards Bray Head and the Little Sugar Loaf from between pine trees at the hillfort site at Rathmichael.

onto a narrow, grassy path with the sea now away to your right.

The path now swings around in a semicircle just south-east of Puck's Castle. Killiney Hill soon appears again through a gap in the trees on the right. As the path veers to the south-east, the Lead Mines Chimney (visited in the next route) can be seen on the hillside ahead. Three Rock Mountain and its masts are visible further away on the right too.

The path gradually ascends to reach the rath by a pocket of pine trees. The rath sits on a flat, grassy mound with splendid 360º views of the surrounding area. The grassy meadow is a fine place to have a picnic and enjoy views across to Bray Head, the Little Sugar Loaf and out to sea.

When ready, follow the broad grassy path down to meet a surfaced, forest track. Turn right on the track to follow the Green Trail as it descends to meet a junction by a signpost.

Leave the Green Trail there, turn right and retrace steps back to the start.

Lead Mines Chimney and Carrickgollogan

A lovely, short walk to a nineteenth-century chimney tower and to a hillock with surprisingly great all-round views.

Grade:	1
Distance:	2.5km (1½ miles)
Ascent:	75m (246ft)
Time:	1–1½ hours
Map:	OSi 1:50,000 Sheet 50

Start/finish: Leave the M50 at Junction 15 towards Cornelscourt/ Kilternan. At the roundabout, take the third exit towards Glenamuck Road. Continue ahead at the next roundabout, taking the first exit. Soon arrive at another roundabout and take the second exit, staying on Glenamuck Road. Continue for around 1.7km. The road narrows at its end to reach a set of traffic lights with The Golden Ball pub ahead. Turn left there onto the Enniskerry Road/R117. Not long after, pass the blue Our Lady of the Wayside church on the right. Ignore the R116 junctions on the right and left and continue ahead. After around 500m from the church, turn left onto Barnaslingan Lane. The narrow road passes large walled estates. It dips and passes a narrow road on the left, then climbs to reach a junction at Barnaslingan Woods. Go left here into a narrow road and continue for around 300m to reach the entrance to Carrickgollogan car park on the left. Car park opening hours are 10 a.m. – 4 p.m. (winter), 10 a.m. – 8 p.m. (summer). For up-to-date opening hours, see: www.dublinmountains.ie/ recreation_sites

In the event that the car park is closed or if there are no spaces available, turn back and park at Barnaslingan Woods.

The Lead Mines Chimney can be seen from the roadside at Stepaside and Kilternan, or from the eastern slopes of Three Rock Mountain. The chimney is a tapered tower, open at the top, and is constructed from large blocks of granite. A stairway of stone blocks spirals up the tower, with some of the lower sections missing. A photo taken in 1900 by Weston Joyce suggests the tower was taller than it is today. Our route begins from the Carrickgollogan Forest Recreation Area car park. Most of it goes through mixed woodlands comprised of beech, birch, cypress, fir, larch

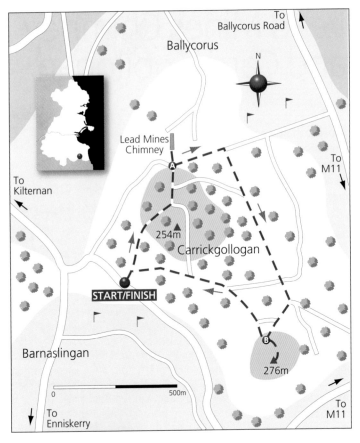

Footprint symbols on a signpost: the Orange Trail, or Lead Mines Way, is our aim for the day.

and pine trees. It visits the chimney and the hillock of Carrickgollogan (276m/905½ft), also known to locals as 'Kattygollogher'. Most of the route is on broad forest tracks except for the short section below the summit of Carrickgollogan. The forest tracks are firm and well-defined, but it does get quite muddy after a wet spell so bring along walking boots or wellies just in case!

Route Description

Take the path to the left of a noticeboard at the rear of the car park towards forest

114

barriers. At a three-way junction, follow orange footprint signs on a firm track ahead. Pass under electric lines before the track climbs gradually uphill.

The track is soon flanked by conifers. Keep a lookout for badgers, rabbits and the native red squirrel in the trees. A good indication of the presence of squirrels is chewed pine or spruce cones on the forest floor. The squirrels normally make chattering noises and spend most of their time foraging in the tree canopy.

Ignore a minor track on the left and continue uphill, still following orange footprint signs, to reach a major junction. Turn left here, only to reach another junction after around 50m.

The Lead Mines Chimney.

Ignore the right branch and continue ahead for another 50m to meet yet another junction (Point A on the map).

The Lead Mines Chimney is now visible ahead. Leave the forest track here and take the obvious, smaller path ahead to reach the chimney. It is possible to enter the tower through an opening to look straight up to its open top.

As you approach the chimney, a path to its left descends to a viewpoint above a rocky slab. The area, around 50m away from the chimney, is surrounded by coconut-scented gorse which blooms yellow over the summer months. There are fine views of the surrounding countryside across to Ballybetagh Woods and down to Ballycorus, Johnstown and Kingston from here.

Just below the slab are the remains of a tunnel, which was connected to an early nineteenth-century lead smelting site in the Ballycorus foothills. The site continued to operate until the 1920s, whisking fumes and smoke from the smelting process up the long tunnel to the chimney, then finally into the atmosphere.

Retrace steps up to the chimney and back to the junction at Point A. Continue eastwards and ahead here on a firm track leading downhill. There are conifers on the right and a field bordered by gorse bushes on the left.

The junction where the Orange and White trails veer left onto a path that leads to the summit of Carrickgollogan.

Looking toward Bray Head and Little Sugar Loaf from the summit of Carrickgollogan.

reach a crossroads with an information board. Continue ahead there along the track which is now flanked by bracken.

Reach a Yellow Man signpost with a minor path to its left. Ignore this and advance to a distinct Y-junction ahead. Veer right here and reach another junction shortly afterwards at **O 231**41 **202**09. The Yellow Man sign points to the right and the orange footprint signs lead left and uphill.

Turn left here to follow the orange footprint signs. The hillock of Carrikgollogan rises ahead. Leave the forest path after around 80m at Point B and veer left onto a narrow, firm and rocky path to the summit. The top is rocky and grassy, and for a low-lying hill it provides fabulous 360° views. Views include Bray Head, the Little Sugar Loaf and Great Sugar Loaf, and the coastline from Wicklow, Killiney, Dublin Bay and as far as Howth. To its opposite side is the sweep of hills from Djouce to Fairy Castle.

The kestrel is a bird of prey that can be commonly spotted from the summit. It has a blue-grey head and tail, and chestnut-brown upper parts with black spots. Boasting a wingspan of up to 82cm, it is the only Irish bird that hovers. During a hunt, the kestrel hovers before pouncing on its prey.

Retrace steps to Point B. Go left, then a few paces afterwards veer right onto a path that leads back to meet the main track again. Turn left there, ignore all junctions and simply follow the track for around 750m back to the Carrickgollogan Forest car park.

Barnaslingan Trail and The Scalp

A pleasant walk through mature woodlands to one of County Dublin's finest viewpoints.	**Grade:** 1
	Distance: 1.75km (1 mile)
	Ascent: 75m (246ft)
	Time: 1 hour
	Map: East West Mapping 1:30,000 *The Dublin Mountains & North Wicklow* or OSi 1:50,000 Sheet 50

Start/finish: Leave the M50 at Junction 15 towards Cornelscourt/ Kilternan. At the roundabout, take the third exit towards Glenamuck Road. Continue ahead at the next roundabout, taking the first exit. Soon arrive at another roundabout and take the second exit, staying on Glenamuck Road. Continue for around 1.7km. The road narrows at its end to reach a set of traffic lights with The Golden Ball pub ahead. Turn left onto the Enniskerry Road/R117. Not long after, pass the blue Our Lady of the Wayside church on the right. Ignore the R116 junctions on the right and left and continue ahead. After around 500m from the church, turn left onto Barnaslingan Lane. The narrow road passes large walled estates. It dips and passes a narrow road on the left, then climbs to reach a junction at Barnaslingan Woods. Use the car park to the right there at the Forest Recreation Area at **O 222**38 **204**31. Opening hours of the car park are: 7 a.m. – 9 p.m. (April– September), 8 a.m. – 5 p.m. (October–March). For up-to-date opening hours see: www.dublinmountains.ie/recreation_sites

The Scalp (*na Scailpe*, 'chasm/cleft') is a glacial overflow channel carved at the end of the last ice age, when a large volume of glacial meltwater was trapped between the mountains and the ice to the north. The water had nowhere to escape so it rose to the top of the Scalp and the force of the gushing water carved out its rocky face. This is best viewed from the glacial spillway along a section of the Enniskerry Road/ R117, just after the former Kilternan Hotel/Ski Club of Ireland buildings. The rocky and boulder-filled west-facing face of the Scalp was popular

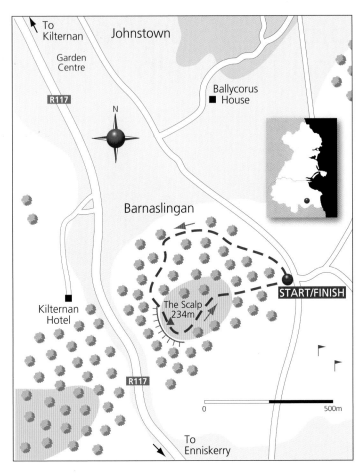

with nineteenth-century Victorian photographers who once came here with their bulky tripods and high-wheeled penny-farthing bicycles. This route starts from the Barnaslingan Woods Forest Recreation Area car park, initially passing through a lovely wooded area dominated by large Corsican pine trees. An easy ascent through woodlands leads to a grassy and rocky clearing on top of the Scalp to reveal spectacular views of the valley below and the Wicklow hills beyond.

Route Description

Go to the rightmost corner of the car park from the entrance to Barnaslingan Woods. There is a white footprint signpost there with a red background. The information board near the front of the car park refers to

Follow Yellow Man symbols on signposts and tree trunks in the woods uphill to the Scalp.

this as the Scalp Lookout Trail. To be consistent with the colouring scheme, let's call this the Red Trail.

Follow a firm track flanked by bracken and pine trees. Ash, holly, oak and sycamore trees blend in with the main canopy of tall pine trees. The path soon bends to the right but keep following Red Trail signposts to reach a gap in a moss-covered stone wall. The track, flanked by bracken slopes, then goes gradually uphill.

The track forks at **O 217**₅₅ **205**₃₂ soon after. The left fork leads uphill while a Yellow Man sign points ahead. Here, veer left and walk uphill following the Red Trail on a broad forest track.

The track soon narrows into a forest path in an area populated with birch trees. Yellow Man signs on the trees guide the way up

Along the Red Trail between tall pine trees in Barnaslingan Woods.

the forest. The signposted path veers right just below an area of bracken. Yellow Man signs lead to a clearing on the right, where there are some mature Scots pine trees.

119

A short detour to the right of the main path leads to a rocky viewpoint at the Scalp clifftop. Here, you can appreciate what fine views it offers. Gaze down into the lush valley below and across to the dense pine woods of Killegar. Then there are the distant vistas of the Wicklow hills and the unmistakable, conical shape of the Great Sugar Loaf to the south/south-west.

Retrace steps back to the main path earlier and continue on until it forks. A Yellow Man sign now points left but you need to follow the Red Trail to the right. The Red Trail signs are mounted on trees and the path goes below a large boulder on the left-hand slope.

The path passes through nineteenth-century woodland dominated by old Scots pine and beech trees. Keep a lookout for birds such as the jay, robin and wood pigeon while walking through the woods.

After crossing a moss-covered stone wall, follow a surfaced forest track to reach a fork. Veer right here, still following Red Trail signs. Pass a wooden bench shortly after, as the track passes under electric lines and leads back to the car park at the start.

The Scalp Lookout point, with the Great Sugar Loaf ahead.

Prince William's Seat and Raven's Rock from Glencullen

A proper family hillwalk with stunning views and giving you the chance to claim an Arderin!

Grade:	3
Distance:	9.5km (6 miles) from Boranaraltry Bridge, 10.75km (6¾ miles) from R116.
Ascent:	320m (1,050ft) from Boranaraltry Bridge, 360m (1,181ft) from R116.
Time:	4–5 hours from Boranaraltry Bridge, 4½–5½ hours from R116.
Map:	East West Mapping 1:30,000 *The Dublin Mountains & North Wicklow* or OSi 1:50,000 Sheet 50 & 56

Start/finish: Leave the M50 at Junction 15 towards Cornelscourt/ Kilternan. At the roundabout, take the third exit towards Glenamuck Road. Continue ahead at the next roundabout, taking the forst exit. Soon arrive at another roundabout and take the second exit, staying on Glenamuck Road. Continue for around 1.7km. The road narrows at its end to reach a set of traffic lights with The Golden Ball pub ahead. Turn left onto the Enniskerry Road/R117 and continue for around 450m to reach a junction just after the blue Our Lady of the Wayside church. Turn right here onto the R116. Pass a school on the right then negotiate some hairpin bends before continuing towards Glencullen. Pass St Patrick's church and Johnnie Fox's Pub to reach Glencullen Crossroads. Continue ahead on the R116 for another 1.6km before turning left into Boranaraltry Lane and descending to the bridge at **O 168**50 **206**00. There are spaces for about four cars in narrow lay-bys on either side of the bridge. If there are no spaces here, head back up Boranaraltry Lane to the R116. Go left at the top of the lane and reach a large car park on the right at **O 172**52 **208**50 after around 150m.

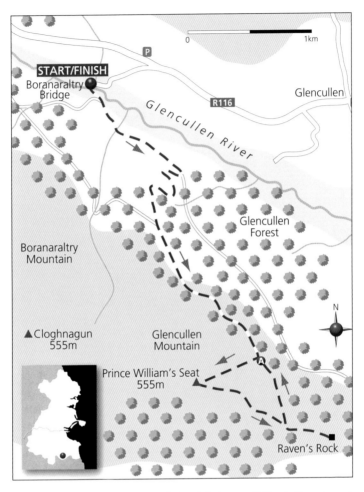

The he origin of the name of the hill, Prince William's Seat, is not entirely certain. It may be linked to the visit of the English monarch King George IV in 1821 or William III around 130 years earlier. Another possibility is the name of a granite tor near its westwards summit of Knocknagun called Fitzwilliam's Seat. This was where men from the Fitzwilliam clan, owners of these uplands in the sixteenth and seventeenth centuries, rested during hunts. The summit of Prince William's Seat (555m/1,821ft) straddles the Dublin/Wicklow county border and is classified by mountainviews.ie as an Arderin – an Irish summit over 500m. To date, there are 407 Arderins listed on mountainviews.ie. This route visits the summit of Prince William's Seat, approaching it from the northern or

*The junction at **O 182**07 **184**65. Take the subsidiary path (left) uphill and a few paces further, look out for a Wicklow Mountains National Park signpost on the left.*

Glencullen (Dublin) side of the hill. It is the most challenging route in this book and gives you the chance to claim an Irish Arderin! A section of the route also crosses into County Wicklow to visit the rugged outcrop of Raven's Rock, where the coastal views from here are even better than from Prince William's Seat, and is very much worth the visit.

Route Description

There are lovely views of the Glencullen River and its surrounding countryside from Boranaraltry Bridge. The bridge was destroyed in a flood on 25 August 1905, but rebuilt four months later. In 2011, the bridge was restored further: it got a new deck and parapet walls were also added.

Ignore a lane to the right going steeply uphill after the bridge. The route forward is indicated by Yellow Man Wicklow Way signposts. Pass a rusted zinc enclosure on the right to reach a metal gate by a stream. Use the swinging metal gate there, then bypass a metal barrier just afterwards on its right.

The tarmac lane soon turns into a broad, gravel track with a grassy centre strip. A fertile, green valley, dotted with houses, stretches to the left below. It is quiet except for the mooing of cows, the trilling of birds and the occasional bark of sheepdogs. Sheep graze in the grassy, stone-walled fields peppered with yellow gorse.

Reach a swinging metal gate at **O 175**25 **199**92. Continue along the forest track to reach a crossroads. Turn right here, still following the Wicklow Way. After a barrier, the track ascends steeply uphill and is flanked by conifers.

Ignore the next junction and continue ahead. The track soon changes from stony to earthen and reaches a large circular area. The broad track

The view down into Glencree and across toward the Tonduffs from Raven's Rock.

soon dwindles to a narrow path and reaches a junction at **O 182**07 **184**65 (Point A on the map) where the Wicklow Way continues towards Ballinultach Forest. The conical shape of the Great Sugar Loaf is prominent ahead and the Lead Mines Chimney can also be seen away to the left.

Here, leave the Wicklow Way and veer right on a subsidiary path uphill. There is a Wicklow Mountains National Park signpost a few paces along this subsidiary path. Veer left here on an informal, earthen path which is boggy in places. With the conifer trees behind, now ascend the heathery and grassy slopes. As height is gained, Fairy Castle, the masts of Three Rock Mountain and the urban sprawl of Dublin city also come into view behind.

Soon the top of Prince William's Seat is reached, marked by a trig pillar amongst a jumble of rocks. Here, the rugged landscape southwards contrasts quite profoundly: from the grey metropolis of Dublin city to the green, rolling hills to the north. The vista to the south is filled by row upon row of higher yellow-brown Wicklow Mountains and interconnecting ridges.

Turn left/south-east on reaching the summit, leave the trig pillar behind and follow a path downhill towards Raven's Rock. The Great Sugar Loaf and the sea are now directly ahead, with the Wicklow Mountains to your right. The path soon meets the Wicklow Way again, which runs perpendicular to it.

Turn right onto the Wicklow Way to shortly reach a Yellow Man signpost where the track forks. Veer left here to follow an informal path at a fence corner. This path, rocky in places and flanked by heathery slopes, gradually rises to reach the granite outcrop of Raven's Rock. The views from the top of the outcrop are impressively wild, especially south towards Knockree Hill, Glencree, Maulin, the Tonduffs and Djouce.

When ready, return to the Wicklow Way. Turn right here and follow the signposts to reach the junction you passed at Point A. Retrace steps from here back to the start.

Three Rock Wood and Three Rock Mountain from Ticknock Lower

Climb Three Rock via quiet mountain trails and enjoy unparalleled views of Dublin city and the sea.

Grade:	2
Distance:	4km (2.5 miles)
Ascent:	180m (591ft)
Time:	1½–2½ hours
Map:	East West Mapping 1:30,000 *The Dublin Mountains & North Wicklow* or OSi 1:50,000 Sheet 50

Start/finish: Leave the M50 at Junction 13 and take the R826 exit for Sandyford/Dundrum. At the roundabout, take the first exit onto the R133. Follow the R133 for 1.3km, then turn left onto Grange Road/R822, following signs for Ticknock. Continue along Grange Road/R822 for 600m, then turn left onto Harold's Grange Road/R113. Follow Harold's Grange Road/R113 for 1km before turning right onto Ticknock Road. Drive along the narrow road for around 1.2km, ignore a junction to the right, and continue for another 300m to reach the entrance for Ticknock Forest. Turn left here into Ticknock Forest. Ignore a junction to the left after 50m. Continue for another 50m beyond that junction to park at spaces at **O 168**₈₈ **242**₂₄ just before a right-hand bend in the road. It can be busy here, especially at weekends. If there are no parking spaces near the entrance, continue beyond the right-hand bend to find more spaces further along the forest road. Note the Ticknock Forest Recreation Area car park closes at 4 p.m. (November–March) and 8 p.m. (April–October). For up-to-date opening hours see: www.dublinmountains.ie/recreation_sites

This route begins from near the entrance of Ticknock Forest which is managed by Coillte through the Dublin Mountains Partnership. Besides a number of signposted walks, there are also a network of mountain bike trails and an orienteering course. This route avoids the busy tarmac road leading up the hillside but uses the Mountain Access Route trail and later the quieter Green Trail that contours along the forested

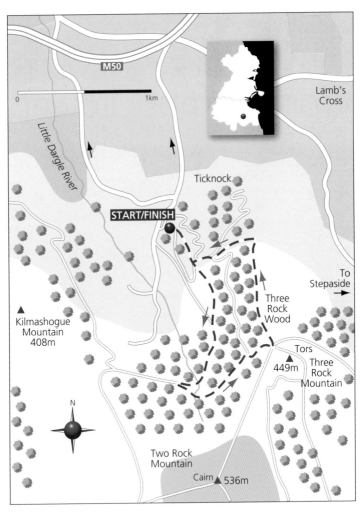

slopes. A short section along the Red Trail leads back to the tarmac road, which culminates on Three Rock Mountain. Three Rock should be renamed 'Mast Mountain' with its television, radio, mobile telephone and emergency service communications masts littered around the summit area. The main transmitting mast is owned by RTÉ, Ireland's national television and radio broadcaster, whose signals have been broadcast from here since 1978. Masts aside, there is no denying the vantage point of the 449m/1,473ft shoulder of Three Rock Mountain, which provides unsurpassed panoramas of Dublin city, harbour and bay to the visitor.

The Mountain Access Route and footprint markers pointing the way uphill at the start of the walk.

Along the Green Trail near the Old Rifle Range, with the Little Dargle Valley on the right and Three Rock Wood ahead.

Route Description

From the parking place at **O 168**₈₈ **242**₂₄, locate the Mountain Access Route trail, signposted by footprint signs to the right of a wooden shed. The narrow, earthen trail is firm underfoot and is flanked by young conifer trees. Follow the trail uphill to reach an arrangement of boulders at a forest road above.

This is the upper section of the one-way looped road beginning and ending at the Ticknock Forest entrance. We will use the parking spaces here for the next route in the book. For now, stop and appreciate the panorama of the Dublin metropolis below to the north/north-east.

Ignore an information board and forest barrier ahead and turn right on the road. After around 50m, leave the road and turn left to follow the Green Trail signposts, designated by white arrows or footprints on a green background.

Cross a forest barrier and follow the trail uphill. The meandering trail is flanked by tall pine trees to reach a broad forest lay-by. A mountain bike track spills down the forested slopes of Three Rock Wood to the left. At a three-way junction, take the middle path to the left of a rusted zinc enclosure.

The path forks shortly after passing the zinc enclosure. Ignore the left fork leading uphill to an unused building. Take the right fork, still following the Green Trail. This is a pleasant stretch: gorse bushes bloom bright yellow in season on grassy slopes to the left; a young conifer forest fills the valley, with Kilmashogue Mountain as the backdrop to its right.

The path climbs gradually uphill and forks by a copse of tall pine trees and a stream, with a line of rocks to its right. Take the left-hand fork uphill to continue following the Green Trail and reach a T-junction.

Leave the Green Trail and turn left along a broad, surfaced track. Follow the meandering track under the cover of pine trees to reach a barrier

Two marked trails near the Dublin Mountains Way wooden post: the Red Trail is for mountain bikers, and the one to its right with the 'no biking' sign is for walkers only.

Expansive views of Dublin city, Howth and Dublin Bay from the Dublin Mountains Way signpost on Three Rock Mountain.

and an information board. Turn right at the junction here onto a broad, surfaced forest road.

Continue uphill and after a bend arrive at a crossroads with some masts looming ahead. There are wooden seats by an information board on the left. Go left at the crossroads. A tall wooden Dublin Mountains Way post stands proudly on the edge of the hillside. Spread out below is the grand panorama of the hillside, flamed with yellow gorse in the summer, and the urban sprawl of Dublin city with views extending as far as Howth and Dublin Bay.

Detour to granite tors: Instead of turning left at the crossroads, continue ahead on the tarmac road for around 150m. At the top of a rise, you will meet a group of three separate granite outcrops to the right of the road. There is another outcrop to the left of the road slightly further on. These distinctive outcrops or tors, are also visited in the next route.

Just before the tall wooden post, there are two waymarked trails on the left: one trail is for mountain bikers and the other for walkers. Ensure that you take the trail for walkers. The trail is firm, earthen and rocky in places and follows the forest boundary of Three Rock Wood to the left.

Descend along the trail to reach the corner of the forest. Here, veer left at the R43 signpost and follow a firm path running along some pine trees. A clearing immediately appears on the right giving more views of Dublin city, Howth and the sea.

Ignore all subsidiary paths to the left and right (these are mountain bike trails). The main path meanders through the trees of Three Rock Wood and soon reaches the forest road. Turn right on the road and pass the forest barrier and information board you saw earlier in the day.

At the T-junction, you arrive at the arrangement of boulders again, at the top of the Mountain Access Route. Here, simply retrace steps back to the start.

Fairy Castle, Two Rock Mountain and Three Rock Mountain from Ticknock Upper

Classic city, coastal and country views and your chance to claim another Irish Arderin.

Grade: Short Option 2, Long Option 3

Distance: Short Option 5.5km (3½ miles); Long Option 7km (4¼ miles)

Ascent: Short and Long Options 210m (689ft)

Time: Short Option 2–3 hours; Long Option 3–4 hours

Map: East West Mapping 1:30,000 *The Dublin Mountains & North Wicklow* or OSi 1:50,000 Sheet 50

Start/finish: Use directions in the previous route to reach the entrance of Ticknock Forest. After around 100m, the road takes a sharp right-hand bend. Follow the one-way forest road uphill. After another 400m, the road bends left, then begins to level. Along the top of the road and after another 150m, reach a junction to the right, marked by information boards. Park at spaces or lay-bys anywhere there at **O 170**₃₃ **239**₉₈. Note the Ticknock Forest Recreation Area car park closes at 4 p.m. (November–March) and 8 p.m. (April–October). For up-to-date opening hours see: www.dublinmountains.ie/recreation_sites

The word *tor* is one of the few Celtic words (Scots Gaelic *'tórr'*, Old Welsh *'twrr'*) borrowed into vernacular English before the modern era. The granite tors on Two Rock and Three Rock Mountains are large outcrops which were eroded over the millennia by the elements. There are double tors on the south-eastern flanks of Two Rock Mountain. Although its highest point is known locally as Fairy Castle (536m/1,759ft), these double tors are what gives the mountain its name. The 'top' marked as Three Rock Mountain (449m/1473ft) is really just a shoulder, but so named in reference to three distinct granite tors found nearby. This route

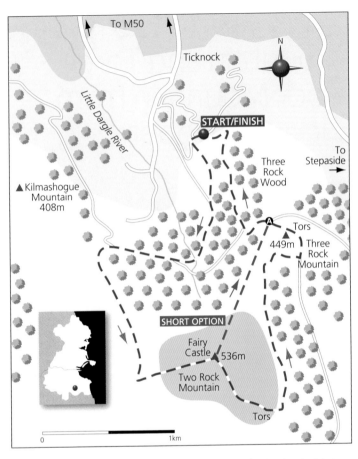

provides two options: the normal route is longer and visits the double tors of Two Rock Mountain. The shorter option makes a beeline down to Three Rock Mountain, bypassing the double tors. Both options include a visit to the triple tors (there is actually another one slightly further on!) of Three Rock Mountain. A further bonus is that the summit of Fairy Castle/Two Rock Mountain is listed as an Irish Arderin – one of 407 Irish summits over 500m.

Route Description – *Long Option*

It might take time just to get going as the bird's-eye view of Dublin city and the sea below will stop you in your tracks. The green countryside, dominated by the Little Dargle Valley in front, with Kilmashogue Mountain to the left, completes the impressive panorama.

Looking towards Dublin city, Dublin Bay and the masts of Three Rock Mountain from the trig pillar and summit cairn of Fairy Castle.

When ready, head southwards from the junction and back along the forest road in the direction you came. After around 50m, leave the road and turn left to follow the Green Trail signposts, designated by white arrow or footprints on a green background.

Cross a forest barrier and follow the trail uphill. The meandering trail is flanked by tall pine trees to reach a broad forest lay-by. A mountain bike track spills down the forested slopes of Three Rock Wood to the left. At a three-way junction, take the middle path to the left of a rusted zinc enclosure.

The path forks shortly after passing the zinc enclosure. Ignore the left fork leading uphill to an unused building. Take the right fork, still following the Green Trail. This is a delightful stretch: gorse bushes bloom bright yellow in season on grassy slopes; a young conifer forest fills the lovely valley, with Kilmashogue Mountain as the backdrop to its right.

The path climbs gradually uphill and forks by a copse of tall pine trees and a stream, with a line of rocks to its right. Take the left fork uphill to continue following the Green Trail and reach a T-junction.

Turn right at the T-junction, still marked by the Green Trail signs. The broad, gravel track now contours along the northern forested slopes of Fairy Castle, with expansive views of Dublin city and the sea below to your right.

After around 500m, reach a broad junction to your left, marked by a red mountain bike trail sign. Ignore this and continue slightly further to reach a path on the left with some large boulders leading up to it. This path is the Green Trail and is also marked by a Yellow Man signpost as it is part of the Wicklow Way.

The path is firm and distinct. It skirts to the right of a forest initially, but then is soon flanked by open hillside, the rugged slopes of which are characterised by grass, gorse and heather. Continue to reach a distinct junction where the Wicklow Way and the Green Trail diverge.

The Green Trail now meets a section of the Dublin Mountain Way. Turn left at the junction and follow the Green Trail. The path is stony and rocky in places and climbs gradually uphill, finally reaching a large cairn and trig pillar on the summit of Fairy Castle *(Sliabh Lecga,* 'mountain of flagstones').

The cairn is a circular structure around 2m high and 20m wide, and is believed by archaeologists to house a megalithic burial chamber. A boardwalk, designed to prevent erosion, circumnavigates the summit area.

The views here are extensive and contrasting. To the north/north-east is the grey, urban sprawl of Dublin city with the red-and-white striped Poolbeg chimneys, Howth Peninsula and islands, and the expanse of blue sea. On the other hand, its southern stretch reveals a vista of wide, green valleys and rolling, brown hills. The highest hills of north Wicklow may be appreciated from here, as well as the distinguished cone of the Great Sugar Loaf.

Short Option: From the way you came and at the summit of Fairy Castle, turn left and descend north-east along an earthen path with scattered rock. The path is initially flanked by heathland before running along the edge of a forest. Keep the trees to your left and take care along the path as it becomes rocky in places. The path soon turns earthen again then broadens into a large, surfaced track to reach the crossroads at Point A (see map and below). From here, you may wish to detour right for 150m to visit the granite tors that give Three Rock Mountain its name.

From the way you came and at the summit of Fairy Castle, veer right and descend south-east along a broad, earthen path which is rocky in places. Now a jumble of boulders can be seen, with the Great Sugar Loaf as the backdrop in the distance. As you approach these boulders, enjoy views across to Glencullen and as far as Kippure.

The path veers left at the boulders then crosses a damaged fence. Ignore subsidiary paths and continue to reach two granite tors at **O 176**18

Views of Dublin city, Howth and Dublin Bay from Three Rock Mountain.

On top of a granite tor on Three Rock Mountain.

219₉₆. Here, the views across to Bray Head, the Little Sugar Loaf and Great Sugar Loaf, and down into Glencullen are even better.

Soon descend a short, eroded section to meet a broad, stony track running perpendicular below. An expanse of conifers blocks any further way forward. Go left here, keeping the trees to your immediate right.

Ignore all subsidiary paths and continue for around 1km to pass two tall transmission masts on the right. At the end of the trees and shortly after passing the second mast, reach a fork at **O 175**₈₆ **230**₅₂. The distinctive group of granite tors marking the shoulder of Three Rock Mountain can be seen away to the right.

We are now heading towards the tors: so veer right, ignore a (right) junction and continue until reaching a broad surfaced track running perpendicular to the path. Here, take a narrow, earthen path directly ahead. The path runs along a fence and passes some masts and a building to meet a broad track. Turn left here, keeping the forest on the right until meeting a broad, surfaced forest track.

The track runs perpendicular to the path. Turn left and after a short rise arrive at the granite tors. There is a large outcrop on the right and three more slightly further along on the opposite side. You may wish to spend some time here at the tors and admire again the expansive view of Dublin city.

When ready, continue along the broad track passing more masts to arrive at a crossroads (Point A). There are wooden benches here and an information board, with more lovely panoramas of the hillside, city and the sea to the right.

Continue ahead there on the tarmac forest road. It conveniently descends the hillside through Three Rock Wood. After one large switchback, a short downhill section leads back to the start.

Tibradden Mountain

Climb above a pine forest to reach a summit with ancient artefacts and rewarding views.	**Grade:**	2
	Distance:	4km (2½ miles)
	Ascent:	170m (558ft)
	Time:	1¾–2¼ hours
	Map:	East West Mapping 1:30,000 *The Dublin Mountains & North Wicklow* or OSi 1:50,000 Sheet 50

Start/finish: Leave the M50 at Junction 12 taking the exit for Knocklyon/ Firhouse/R113. Keep left at the fork, following signs for Scholarstown/ Ballyboden/R113. On reaching a roundabout, take the second exit onto Scholarstown Road. At the next roundabout, take the third exit to stay on Scholarstown Road. Continue for around 800m then turn right onto Edmondstown Road/R116. Follow the R116 for around 4.5km to reach a T-junction. Take a sharp left towards Glencullen there. The entrance to Tibradden Forest is on your left at **O 139**₀₀ **227**₀₀ around 150m further.

Parking Information: Tibradden Forest car park is open weekends and bank holidays only from 10 a.m. – 4 p.m. (March – October). It is closed from November to February. If the car park is closed, there are limited spaces before the forest barrier. For up-to-date opening hours see: www. dublinmountains.ie/recreation_sites

It is useful to check the Zipit opening times in the summer season (www.zipit.ie) as its car park might be open to accommodate.

The south Dublin area on the borderland of the Pale was once known as Harold's Country. Its name originated from a wealthy family that lived in the area and left their mark on a number of localities in Dublin such as Harold's Cross and Harold's Grange. Tibradden or *Tigh Bródáin* ('house of Bruadain') is one of the many hills rising south of Harold's Country. Sandwiched between Cruagh Mountain and Kilmashogue Mountain, it rises to 467m/1,532ft above a lovely forested area known as the Pine Forest. Other trees such as beech, oak, larch and spruce are also

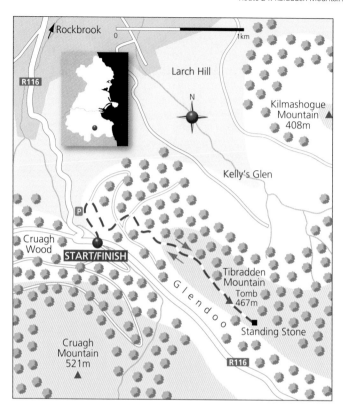

Zip lines at the Zipit Adventure park in Tibradden pine forest at the start of the walk.

Looking north across Kelly's Glen toward Kilmashogue Mountain and Dublin city from the stone circle on Tibradden Mountain.

135

found in the forest. Sightings of badgers, foxes and Sika deer are also quite common in these parts. This is a there-and-back route to a standing stone just beyond the summit of Tibradden Mountain, starting and finishing at the forest car park. You might be tempted to continue along the path for around 750m beyond the standing stone to reach a T-junction where the Dublin Mountain Way and Wicklow Way diverge. But note, as tempting as it may seem, do not attempt to descend to Glendoo via the Wicklow Way and loop back along the R116 to the start. The R116 is a busy road with no verges and is unsafe for children and even adults. Note also the path a few hundred metres north of Tibradden denoted by the double dashed black line in the East West Mapping map is completely overgrown at the time of writing and thus unsuitable for children.

Route Description

Follow the Yellow Man Dublin Mountain Way signposts towards the Zipit Forest Adventure buildings. The aerial circuits composed of zip lines, swings and cargo nets can be seen in the treetops above. Take the Tibradden Mountain Trail (Red Trail) at the end of the car park where the Yellow Man sign points right and uphill.

Standing stone on Tibradden Mountain.

The trail winds up the Pine Forest to reach a broad track above. Turn left there, then take an immediate right onto a path leading uphill, shortly meeting another broad, surfaced forest track.

Go left here onto the broad track following the Yellow Man and Red/White Trail signs. After around 50m, veer right at a junction as directed by a Yellow Man sign placed on a tree.

The surfaced track soon dwindles to an earthen path beyond a jumble of boulders and an information board. It emerges above the treeline and onto the open hillside whose slopes are rich with heather and gorse. A boardwalk is installed along some sections to protect the hillside from further erosion.

The path goes up a moderately steep slope, and then follows the broad crest of its south-east ridge. The bedrock of Tibradden Mountain is composed mainly of granite as evidenced by the granite boulders strewn along its steep, southern slopes.

Looking down on Gleneddy and the Hell Fire Club from the Tibradden Mountain trail above the Pine Forest.

Finally, a stone circle is reached at **O 148**58 **222**65. This consists of a tomb and an inscribed stone, which marks the highest point on Tibradden Mountain. This site is of archaeological importance and a burial urn taken from it is housed in the National Museum in Dublin.

Take your time to appreciate the fine scenery from here. The eye is immediately drawn to Glendoo Valley below to the west and south, guarded by the rugged slopes of Cruagh Mountain and Glendoo Mountain. The landscape to the north is far less intimidating, with pockets of bright green fields, dark green forestry and the solitary Kilmashogue Mountain punctuating the skyline. Behind this is the large, grey sprawl of Dublin city and blue sea. To the north-east and south-east are the rounded, heathery dome of Fairy Castle and the conical profile of the Great Sugar Loaf in the distance.

When ready, continue on for around 200m beyond the stone circle along the broad ridge to reach a standing stone. Like the stone circle, the standing stone is an artefact from the mountain's ancient past.

This is the turn-back point, so retrace steps from here along the ridge via the stone circle. Walking a route in reverse often provides a different perspective, so enjoy the lingering views of the city and its countryside, including the forested landscape away to Montpelier Hill and the Hell Fire Club.

Reach the boardwalk again and retrace steps from there down into the Pine Forest and back to the start.

Cruagh Mountain Loop

A broad summit with commanding views of Dublin city. Best climbed in the summer when its slopes are a feast of pink, purple and yellow!	**Grade:**	2
	Distance:	5km (3 miles)
	Ascent:	160m (525ft)
	Time:	2–3 hours
	Map:	East West Mapping 1:30,000 *The Dublin Mountains & North Wicklow* or OSi 1:50,000 Sheet 50

Start/finish: Leave the M50 at Junction 12 taking the exit for Knocklyon/ Firhouse/R113. Keep left at the fork, following signs for Scholarstown/ Ballyboden/R113. On reaching a roundabout, take the second exit onto Scholarstown Road. At the next roundabout, take the third exit to stay on Scholarstown Road. Continue for around 800m then turn right onto Edmondstown Road/R116. Follow the R116 for around 4.5km to reach a T-junction. Turn right here and continue for around 1km on Cruagh Road to reach the Cruagh Wood forest recreation area car park on the left at **O 127**42 **226**10. Opening times: 7 a.m. – 9 p.m. (April–September), 8 a.m. – 5 p.m. (October–March). If the car park is closed or if there are no more spaces available, park with consideration on the inner side of the road along its verge. For up-to-date opening hours see: www.dublinmountains. ie/recreation_sites

Cruagh Mountain (*Sliabh na Craobhaí,* 'the mountain of the large tree') sprawls above the foothills of Jamestown in south Dublin. Historical records show that Prince John, son of Henry II, granted Cruagh or *Creevagh* with its churches to the See of Dublin in 1184. Prior to that, there was no mention of Cruagh at all. Cruagh Mountain is one of three summits in the area, the other two being Killakee Mountain and Glendoo Mountain. It is essentially a mass of granite bedrock coated with gorse and heather, and stands 521m (1,709ft) above sea level. Its summit area is broad and offers commanding views over the Dublin metropolis. The initial and final parts of the walk pass through dense woodlands comprising of pine

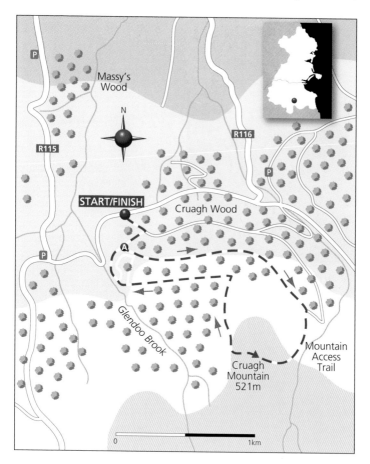

trees, beech, Japanese larch, Norway spruce and Sitka spruce. The well-maintained Cruagh Mountain Access Trail makes it easy to gain the upper slopes of the mountain, from which its summit cairn can be reached. Note the descent route is a plethora of forest tracks and junctions and requires basic navigational skills until meeting the metal ladder stile of the Dublin Mountain Way.

Route Description

It will be difficult to ignore the magnificent panorama of Dublin city to the north from the parking place. When ready, enter Cruagh Wood via the forest barrier near the entrance of the car park. Soon meet another barrier with a signboard and a picnic table nearby.

Rock steps on the signposted Mountain Access Trail

The open hillside of Cruagh Mountain coloured by purple heather and yellow gorse in the summer.

A broad track leads uphill through the forest, soon meeting a junction. The way forward is marked by footprint symbols on a post. Turn right here at the junction and reach another large switchback slightly higher. Veer left at the switchback (Point A on the map), still following the same footprint symbols and also Yellow Man signs as you now meet the Dublin Mountain Way.

Ignore a junction to the right after around 50m beyond the switchback. Continue ahead until the broad track levels off in an area flanked by conifers. A clearing soon appears on the left giving fine views of Dublin city and the sea.

The Cruagh Mountain Access Trail is soon reached on the right, designated by a signboard at its base. Leave the broad forest track and turn right, initially up rocky steps and then on the boardwalk of the Access Trail. The boardwalk was constructed by volunteers of Mountain Meitheal in conjunction with the Dublin Mountains Partnership and Coillte. It leads uphill and above the treeline.

Emerge on the open hillside, the slopes of which are blanketed in heather and gorse. It is a feast of colours, particularly over the summer months, with the heather flowering pink-purple and the gorse blooming bright yellow.

It is common to spot red grouse (*Cearc fhraoigh*, 'bird of heather') here during its breeding season from February to March, but be warned – they take flight like a gunshot in a series of explosive wingbeats when disturbed. Smaller than a pheasant, the male grouse sports a red-brown plumage, whereas its female counterpart has a yellower plumage. You can sometimes hear their call, a series of loud nasal sounds ending in a piercing trill.

Turn right at the top of the Access Trail and almost immediately after veer left onto a narrow path to reach the corner of a fence. There is a cairn not far from here at **O 137**₀₃ **216**₈₂. Walk to the cairn, a small pile of rocks, which marks the summit of Cruagh Mountain.

The view northwards from the cairn towards Dublin city is especially commanding. On a clear day it is possible to distinguish prominent landmarks such as the Wellington Monument in the Phoenix Park, the green dome of the Four Courts, the Spire, Croke Park and the Aviva Stadium. The twin chimneys of Poolbeg are also visible and so is the headland of Howth.

Cruagh Woods.

From the cairn, descend west on a heathery slope towards some conifer trees. After around 150m, meet a firm path down the slope and turn right onto it. Follow the path for around 500m to meet a broad, distinct track running perpendicular to it.

Turn left onto the broad track and follow it. Ignore two subsidiary tracks to the right. The main track is flanked by tall conifers. Around 700m further, a distinct junction appears on the right. Around 50m after this junction, the main track veers right through a gap in the trees (Grid ref: **O 126**₉₀ **221**₀₄).

Here, leave the main track and take a narrow path on the left. The gorse-lined path follows a fence on the left and the forest boundary to its right. It descends to meet another path with a metal ladder stile nearby.

Turn right along the path and walk away from the stile, following the Yellow Man Dublin Mountain Way signs. This is a delightful stretch, passing under the canopy of tall pine trees.

The switchback at Point A passed earlier in the day is soon reached. Turn left there and retrace steps back to the start.

Massy's Wood

Encounter trees from all over the world in a wooded, eighteenth-century estate.	**Grade:**	1
	Distance:	3km (2 miles)
	Ascent:	Negligible
	Time:	1–1½ hours
	Map:	East West Mapping 1:30,000 *The Dublin Mountains & North Wicklow* or OSi 1:50,000 Sheet 50

Start/finish: Leave the M50 at Junction 12 and head towards Firhouse/ R113. Continue along the R113 to reach a set of traffic lights. Go left there following signs for the Hell Fire Club. Continue ahead at two roundabouts to reach a crossroads. Turn left at the crossroads, followed by a right at a T-junction. Continue uphill along the Old Military Road/R115. After passing the Country Store & Cafe Timbertrove and the entrance to Massy's Wood, reach a car park on the right for the Hell Fire Club at **O 120**₈₅ **237**₆₅. The car park opening hours are: 7 a.m. – 9 p.m. (April–September), 8 a.m. – 5 p.m. (October–March). For up-to-date opening hours see: www. dublinmountains.ie/recreation_sites

The 114 acres (46 hectares) of woodlands of Massy's Estate is now fully managed by Coillte. The original estate, purchased by a rich Dubliner, Luke White, in 1752, encompassed a larger area of 2,903 acres (1,175 hectares). During Cromwellian times, the land descended on the female side of the family to Baron Massy. The Massy family was heavily indebted by 1915. In 1924, the 8th Baron Massy, Hugh Hamon, was evicted from Killakee House by force and deposited at the estate gateway on the public road, somewhere near where the Country Store & Cafe Timbertrove stands today. This walk is an educational nature trail within the mature woodlands of Massy's Estate, with the opportunity to view tree species originating from as far away as Asia and America. The trail later runs along Glendoo Brook, an idyllic section with ponds and miniature falls, before passing through an old walled garden to reach a disused icehouse.

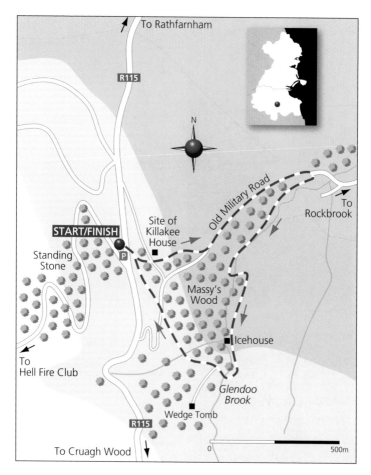

Route Description

Walk out of the Hell Fire Club car park onto the R115. Turn left at the road and go back in the direction of Dublin. After around 100m, arrive at a forest barrier opposite a large red-walled bungalow.

The barrier is the entrance to the Massy's Estate Forest Recreation Area. Walk past a signboard on the left onto a forest track. The track meanders under a thick canopy of trees. Around 100m from the barrier, the track forks and a White/Orange Trail signpost points to the left.

Go left and head downhill to an area with two large uprooted trees. Leave the track here and veer left. The path passes the site of the former Massy Estate House, which was demolished in 1941 following the demise of

143

Along the track near the entrance of Massy's Wood.

The giant sequoia near the former Massy Estate House.

the estate. The forest path reaches a giant sequoia (*Sequoiadendron giganteum*) soon after, followed by a stand of Norway spruce (*Picea abies*), native of Central/Northern Europe.

Soon arrive at a T-junction where the path meets a broad, well-defined forest track. Take a left here, following the Orange Trail to pass an area of oak trees planted by the Ballyroan Boys National School during Tree Week 2004. The track is soon flanked by a deer fence.

Reach a broad lay-by with an entrance into a field to the left. A huge sessile oak (*Quercus petraea*) is found here. Later, a stream can be heard away to the right, after an area of birch trees. The stream – the Glendoo Brook – originates from the heights of White Sands Mountain away to the south.

A wall soon appears on the left. Follow the track around a bend to reach a junction at the end of the wall. Veer right before a forest barrier, still following the Orange/White Trail, to pass under a huge Monterey pine (*Pinus radiata*). The stream now flows to the left of the track.

The trail soon dwindles to a narrow path and follows the stream. This is an interesting section as the path passes a variety of trees. First up is the yew (*Taxus baccata*), then the western red cedar (*Thuja plicata*), native of western North America, and finally the West Himalayan spruce (*Picea smithiana*), native of Afghanistan/Nepal. Slightly further, the European larch (*Larix deciduas*) native of Central Europe can be found, followed by the Norway spruce again.

The path reaches a circular area where there are more western red cedar trees. The Bhutan pine (*Pinus wallichiana*) and rhododendrons from Asia can also be found near the stream.

The arched wall and trail signpost at Massy's Wood.

Disused icehouse, Massy's Wood.

Reach a junction where a Lawson cypress (*Chamaecyparis lawsoniana*) tree, native of north-west California/south-west Oregon, grows by the stream. Ignore the junction to the right and continue along the path by the stream until a wooden fence appears.

Here, veer left and follow the White Trail across the stream. After a bend, the path passes under an arched wall. Go under the arch then turn right, still following the White/Orange Trail signs. The wall is now to your right and the path eventually meets a junction.

Turn right at the junction and walk under another arch, still following the White/Orange Trail signs. The stream now runs to the right and the track rises gradually uphill. It soon passes a disused icehouse on the right. This is a small, cool cavern that was used to store lamb shared by the local community in the past.

The trail then passes large sycamore (*Acer pseudoplatanus*) trees, native to central and southern Europe, at the end of a wall. A clearing is soon reached on the left, giving views beyond a grassy field of the countryside, Dublin city and the sea.

Continue following the trail markers to reach a T-junction. Turn right here following the 'Exit' sign, pass a ruined building on the left and cross a bridge over the Glendoo Brook.

Continue along the main track and ignore all junctions on the left. The track passes a noble fir (*Abies procera*), a native of North America. Beech trees also grow in abundance in the area.

Cross a bridge over another stream. Keep a lookout for the hawthorn (*Crataegus monogyna*) just before the track splits into three. Follow the Orange Trail signpost there and continue straight ahead to reach the forest entrance by the R115.

Turn left on the road and retrace steps back to the car park.

Hell Fire Club

Visit Dublin's 'haunted house' on the hill.	**Grade:**	2
	Distance:	3.5km (2¼ miles)
	Ascent:	100m (328ft)
	Time:	1½–2 hours
	Map:	East West Mapping 1:30,000 *The Dublin Mountains & North Wicklow* or OSi 1:50,000 Sheet 50

Start/finish: Leave the M50 at Junction 12 and head towards Firhouse/ R113. Continue along the R113 to reach a set of traffic lights. Go left here following signs for the Hell Fire Club. Continue ahead at two roundabouts to reach a crossroads. Turn left at the crossroads, followed by a right at a T-junction. Continue uphill along the Old Military Road/R115. After passing the Country Store & Cafe Timbertrove and the entrance to Massy's Wood, reach a car park on the right for the Hell Fire Club at **O 120**₈₅ **237**₆₅. The car park opening hours are: 7 a.m. – 9 p.m. (April–September), 8 a.m. – 5 p.m. (October–March). For up-to-date opening hours see: www. dublinmountains.ie/recreation_sites

The Hell Fire Club is the traditional name given to the 383m (1,257ft) summit of Montpelier Hill which overlooks the Orlagh foothills. The hill takes its name from the ruined building at the summit. Montpelier House, later known as the Hell Fire Club, was originally built as a hunting lodge around 1725 by the Speaker of the Irish House of Commons, William Conolly. He originally named the building 'Mount Pelier' but it was only in the years following his passing in 1729 that the hill's association with the Hell Fire Club started. A group of barons, earls and lords formed a member-only establishment, the aforementioned Hell Fire Club, and used the building to convene from 1735–1741. Evidence of the existence of the club can be found in a painting by James Worsdale, now held by the National Gallery of Ireland. It is said that members, whose club mascot was a black cat, left an empty chair at meetings for the Devil and drank *scaltheen*, a drink made from mixing whiskey and hot butter. At one time, the lodge was damaged by fire, and the club members relocated

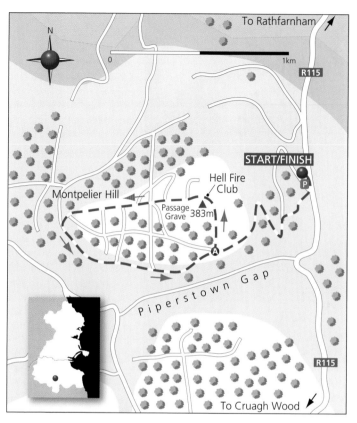

The large boulder and wooden fence near the entrance of the car park. The white footprint symbols of the Blue and Green Trails point the way forward.

to Stewards House along the Military Road for a brief period. The land around the Hell Fire Club was sold to Luke White in 1800, then passed on to the Massy family before being acquired by the Irish State. Today, the area is maintained by Coillte.

Route Description

There is a large boulder and wooden signboard/fence near the entrance of the car park. Follow the Blue/Green Trail signs. Veer left shortly when the trail forks.

147

Under tall pine trees along the broad forest track leading up to the Hell Fire Club.

The trail is a firm, narrow and distinct path flanked by tall gorse bushes, thistles, young Douglas fir and Sitka spruce. It winds uphill to meet a broad, surfaced forest track. The view of the surrounding countryside and the metropolis of Dublin improve as height is gained.

Turn left at the forest track and keep following the Blue/Green Trail. The track climbs uphill under tall pine trees in a series of switchbacks. When the track begins to straighten, a clearing is soon reached on the left giving views south towards Piperstown Gap, Killakee, Featherbed Forest and the hills beyond.

Soon after passing the clearing at **O 116**₃₃ **234**₂₅, the track splits into three (Point A on the map). Ignore the broad forest tracks to the left and ahead. Instead, veer right on a dirt track uphill.

The track tops out on a broad, flat grassy area. The trig pillar marking the summit of the Hell Fire Club and its ruined building can be seen not far away. Slightly beyond the ruined building is a broad, grassy shoulder, ideal for a picnic. Below are the green foothills of Orlagh, Mount Venus and Woodtown; but it is the grand panorama of Dublin city and the sea beyond that captivates the eye.

A cairn with an ancient passage grave used to rest on the summit, and stones from it were used to construct the Hell Fire Club building. However, a fierce storm blew its roof off soon after, leading the locals to believe this to be the work of the paranormal, as retribution for interfering with the burial site.

Rich folklore also haunts the building. One tale speaks of a priest who visited the building at night and discovered its club members partaking in the sacrifice of a black cat. The priest seized the cat and performed an exorcism, upon which a demon was released. Another tale revolves

Trig pillar and the Hell Fire Club building on the summit of Montpelier Hill.

around a stranger who joined the club members in a card game on a stormy night. When a member bent under the table to pick up a dropped card, he noticed the stranger had a cloven hoof!

When ready, with Dublin city behind you, walk across the front of the building to a large rock nearby on its right. A broad track beyond the rock leads westwards and downhill. A Blue Trail signpost sits to the right of the track by the corner of spruce trees.

Ignore all forest tracks to the left and right, and continue ahead. The track passes another Blue Trail signpost and an information board. The track is flanked by conifers and reaches a clearing on the right giving views down into Dublin city once again.

After another signpost, the track descends to reach a T-junction where the Blue and Green Trails diverge. Go left to follow the Blue Trail and soon reach a clearing on the right with fine vistas down into Piperstown Glen

View of Dublin city from the Hell Fire Club.

and the hills beyond. Kippure Mountain can also be seen in the distance.

After the clearing, the track is flanked once again by conifers. It climbs steadily uphill to the junction passed earlier at Point A. Turn right here and retrace steps back to the start.

Glenasmole Reservoirs Loop

A straightforward walk through one of County Dublin's most scenic reservoir-filled valleys.

Grade:	2
Distance:	9km (5½ miles)
Ascent:	70m (230ft)
Time:	3¼–4¼ hours
Map:	East West Mapping 1:30,000 *The Dublin Mountains & North Wicklow* or OSi 1:50,000 Sheet 50

Start/finish: Leave the M50 at Junction 12 and head in the Knocklyon/ R113 direction. At a crossroads with traffic lights, continue ahead. Keep straight ahead at two roundabouts until reaching Oldbawn Crossroads. Turn left here onto the R114. Ignore a left fork into Piperstown around 500m afterwards and continue ahead towards Ballinascorney. Just under another 1.5km the road takes a sharp bend to cross the Dodder River at a narrow bridge. Around 100m after the bend, turn left into Glenasmole car park at **O 089**₁₆ **243**₅₈.

Opening times:
1 April to 30 September: Monday–Friday 8 a.m. – 8 p.m.,
Saturday 1 p.m.–8 p.m., Sunday/Bank Holidays 10 a.m. – 8 p.m;
1 October to 31 March: Monday–Wednesday 8 a.m. – 4.30 p.m.,
Thursday–Friday 8 a.m. – 3.30 p.m., Saturday – closed, Sunday/Bank Holidays 2 p.m. – 5 p.m.
For up-to-date opening hours see:
www.dublinmountains.ie/recreation_sites

In the early twentieth century, the edges of the Glenasmole valley were barren and devoid of trees. Today, thanks to various tree-planting projects and natural colonisation, its lower slopes are filled with ash, birch, hazel, larch, fir, Scots pine and sycamore trees. Glenasmole houses two Bohernabreena reservoirs built from 1883–1887 in its valley floor. The reservoirs once supplied water to the Rathmines township until the 1930s. Both reservoirs are now managed by Dublin City Council, supplying

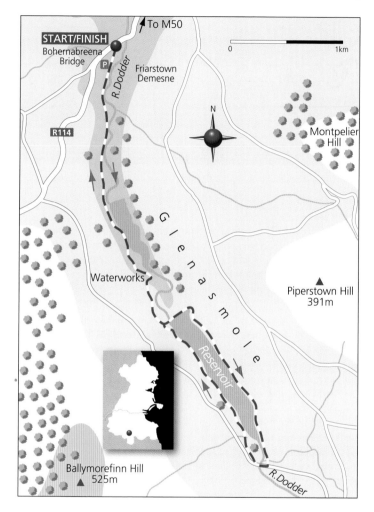

water to nearly 35,000 households in Dublin south. The reservoirs are also a popular spot for brown trout fishing, allowed with a permit only from Dublin City Council or as a member of the Dublin Trout Anglers or Dodder Anglers Club. The lower reservoir is stocked every year with trout, whose sizes range from 0.5–4.5lb. The trout in the upper reservoir are smaller in size but more abundant. Our route approaches the reservoirs from the north: first along a tarmac road towards the lower reservoir, then looping around the upper reservoir before retracing steps back to the start.

Looking south-east along the first and smaller of the two reservoirs in Glenasmole.

Route Description

Enter the smaller metal gate beside the main gate at the reservoir entrance. Follow a tarmac road flanked by trees and bushes, with the Dodder River flowing beyond a fence to the left. Orange Trail and Yellow Man Dublin Mountain Way signs point the way forward. Pass a farmhouse on the right shortly after the trail markers.

Later, the road forks after passing two cottages on the left. Take the right-hand fork and go uphill to arrive at the first and smaller of the two reservoirs. This lower reservoir was traditionally used for flood control or to supply the numerous mills further downstream. There were once over forty mills served by the Dodder – the majority of which were flour mills, but there were also some cotton, dye, glue, paint, paper and saw mills.

If you wish, veer left and walk across a grassy strip along the top of the dam to enjoy views back down the valley and on its opposite end along the reservoir. When ready, head back to the road. Turn left and follow it with the reservoir now to your left.

After the end of the reservoir, the road takes a series of small switchbacks to arrive at a junction with the waterworks building ahead. A Tree of Hope is planted at the junction here as a symbol to all affected by suicide or mental health issues. A sign for the upper reservoir points uphill also.

Turn right and follow Orange Trail/Yellow Man signposts uphill along the broad gravel track. The track leads to the larger of the two reservoirs. This upper reservoir provides cleaner drinking water from the peat-free streams of Featherbed to the east. An impressive overflow system exists here, which allows 1,500 cubic feet of water per minute to pass into a pipeline linked into the natural river channel below the dam. The surplus water is diverted into the lower reservoir where it is held until required.

Veer left and walk along a grassy strip that runs along the top of the dam. The grassy strip is flanked by a stone wall on the right and a fence on the left. The valley to the left is a picturesque scene, dotted with lovely Scots pine trees. Views of the reservoir to the right are good too, with Ballymorefinn Hill rising to the south-west.

Continue to reach the opposite end of the reservoir. Here, with the reservoir now away to your right, a surfaced track undulates under the cover of trees. The shallow ends of the reservoir are colonised by reeds and willows. Keep an eye out for birds such as the heron, dipper, kingfisher and grey wagtail here. On the foothills above the eastern shore of the reservoir are the ruins of St Sentan's – a sixteenth-century church named after a Saxon king's son.

There are two places along the track to approach the water's edge through an obvious clearing in the trees. You may choose to linger by the water to soak in the tranquillity of the surrounding countryside.

When ready, get back on the track and follow it beyond the southern end of the reservoir to reach a metal gate. Bypass the gate to its right and cross a stone bridge. Follow Orange Trail markers and go through a swinging metal gate to arrive at a road.

Turn right on the road and cross a bridge over the River Dodder. Veer right soon after the bridge and enter a metal gate. Follow a broad track beyond the gate. The track meanders along a stream and an artificially constructed stone-faced channel on its left.

The water in this channel is sourced from the slopes of Kippure Mountain and has a high peat content. It bypasses the upper reservoir in a canal and flows down to the Lower Reservoir via the channel.

It's a pleasant stroll along the track and soon the upper reservoir appears again on the right. Follow the track to reach a bridge that crosses the canal and arrive back at the dam on the northern end of the reservoir.

Retrace steps from there back to the start.

The view northward into the valley and the woods at Glenasmole from the top of its upper reservoir.

The view north-west along the water's edge of the upper reservoir from its eastern end near St Sentan's.

Ballymorefinn Hill and Seahan Circuit

Claim your first Vandeleur-Lynam summit and enjoy far-reaching views of city, hills and plains.

Grade:	3
Distance:	7km (4¼ miles)
Ascent:	260m (853ft)
Time:	3–4 hours
Map:	East West Mapping 1:30,000 *The Dublin Mountains & North Wicklow* or OSi 1:50,000 Sheet 50 &56

Start/finish: Leave the M50 at Junction 12 and head in the Knocklyon/R113 direction. At a crossroads with traffic lights, continue ahead. Keep straight ahead at two roundabouts until reaching Oldbawn Crossroads. Turn left here onto the R114. Ignore a left fork into Piperstown around 500m afterwards and continue ahead towards Ballinascorney. After just under another 1.5km, the road takes a sharp bend to cross the Dodder River at a narrow bridge. Ignore all subsidiary junctions afterwards and stay on the R114 for another 2.5km to reach a junction to the left with a stone cross (*c.* 1850). Leave the R114 there and veer left onto the narrow road. Follow the road uphill for around 2km to park on a lay-by on the right opposite a barrier at Seahan Forest (Grid ref: **O 076**$_{00}$ **207**$_{80}$).

Seahan Forest is the gateway to a range of hills rising above Glenasmole Valley to the east. We visit two of these hills in this route: Ballymorefinn Hill (525m/1,722ft) and Seahan (647m/2,123ft). Seahan is a hill of note as it is classed as a Vandeleur-Lynam and Arderin by mountainviews.ie. We explained what an Arderin is earlier in the book. A Vandeleur-Lynam is another list of hills in Ireland that are classified as being over 600m high. There are 273 Vandeleur-Lynam summits in Ireland and this route provides the opportunity to bag your first! Its proximity to Dublin city, broad forest tracks and upland paths makes the circuit easily doable during long summer daylight hours. However, the colours of the hillside are best in spring and autumn. Note: in the winter, there is a chance that the upper slopes of Ballymorefinn Hill and Seahan may get some snow.

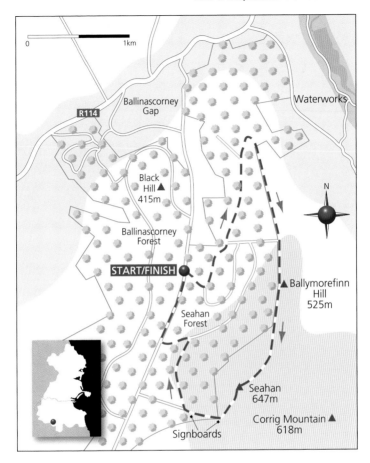

Route Description

Follow a broad, surfaced forest track beyond the barrier to reach a T-junction. Turn left here to continue along the forest track. The track crosses a stream that leads gradually downhill. It passes a grassy firebreak on the left, then a large area of felled trees on the right before the track forks.

A clearing to the left provides fine views of the surrounding countryside towards Ballinascorney. The large sprawl of Dublin city can also be seen ahead. Take the right-hand fork here and continue for around 150m.

Before reaching the end of the broad forest track (Grid ref: **O 081**87 **220**35), veer right onto an informal earthen path through an area of felled trees. The path, which can be indistinct at times, climbs uphill to reach a fence. A rusted metal pole and some rocks are in place to assist with crossing the fence.

The view northwards down Ballymorefinn Hill, with the Glenasmole Valley to the right below and Dublin city in the distance.

The grassy stretch of Ballymorefinn Hill can now be seen ahead, running along a line of conifer trees to its right. Keep a fence to your right and follow the broad, grassy path uphill. As height is gained, the tree-lined Glenasmole Valley and its reservoir appear to the left below. There are also fabulous views of Dublin city behind.

The slope relents after you pass a large boulder. The path is now grassy and earthen with a strip of heather running in the middle. Soon, vistas to the right open up to reveal the countryside towards Saggart Hill and its masts. The summit of Seahan also rises ahead, along with the sweep of the barren brown hillside towards Corrig to its left.

After passing the last line of trees, the path broadens into a stony, rocky track and the slope steepens again. Follow a fence to its corner, ignore a junction on the right, followed by a narrow path on the left and continue straight uphill.

The summit of Seahan (*Suíochán*, 'seat'), with its trig pillar, perched on top of an ancient stone cairn (Grid ref: **O 081**23 **196**98), is soon reached. There are some stone slabs around the summit area that edge a round barrow, within which are the remains of a megalithic tomb. Seahan's higher neighbour, Seefingan (726m/2,382ft), can also be seen to the south ahead.

There are fabulous views from the summit in all directions: to the west are the plains of Brittas and Manor Kilbride; to the south-west sit the Blessington Reservoirs; to the east and south are the summits of Corrig, Seefingan and Seefinn; farther away to the east and north-east the line of the Dublin Mountains.

Descend to the south-west by way of a broad, eroded track at a metal pole. Follow the track down to reach the corner of a young conifer plantation. There are two signboards here: one a military firing range

The view westwards from the trig pillar on the summit of Seahan.

board and another prohibiting the use of quad bikes, mountain bikes and off-road bikes. Ignore a track on the right but descend along a stony and rocky path to the left.

Signboards at the corner of a young conifer plantation on the descent from Seahan: a military firing range board and another one prohibiting the use of bikes.

The path runs alongside a fence to reach another military firing range signboard on the left after around 130m. Leave the track there and turn right onto an earthen path flanked by young conifers beyond a fence there. A plastic tube put in place along a section of fence makes it easy to cross it.

Descend along the path where it soon veers right onto a broad, forest track after a bend. Continue along the forest track until reaching a T-junction. There has been some large-scale tree felling here.

Turn left at the T-junction and continue to reach some beehive-shaped cairns. Arrive at a road after passing a metal forest barrier with a wooden stile to its right.

Turn right on the road as it dips and leads back to the start.

Saggart Hill

An easy climb to reach the top of a hill overlooking the plains of Kildare.	**Grade:**	2
	Distance:	4km (2½ miles)
	Ascent:	100m (328ft
	Time:	1½–2 hours
	Map:	East West Mapping 1:30,000 *The Dublin Mountains & North Wicklow* or OSi 1:50,000 Sheet 50

Start/finish: Leave the M50 at Junction 11 and take the N81 exit towards Tallaght. Continue along the N81 in the direction of Saggart/ Brittas/Blessington. Ignore the Saggart junction and continue along the N81 to pass St Brigid's Nursing Home on the left. After a few bends, the N81 straightens. Around 1.2km after passing St Brigid's, leave the N81 and turn right along a narrow road following signs for Slade Valley Golf Club/Brittas Montessori. Arrive at a crossroads after 250m and turn right there. Follow the road uphill for around 1.1km to reach a lay-by on the left before a forest barrier (Grid ref: **O 023**$_{77}$ **234**$_{93}$). There are spaces for three to four cars.

This is an easy circuit following broad forest tracks to the mast-filled summit and around the forested slopes of Saggart Hill. The Irish of Saggart Hill, *Cnoc Theach Sagard*, means 'hill of the house of Sacra'. Geologically, Saggart Hill, also known as Slievethoul (*Sliabh Toll*), was formed from glacial deposits of sandstone, shale and siltstone laid down at the end of the last ice age. Today, its 397m/1,302ft flat-topped summit is littered with a collection of telecommunications masts. The masts overshadow an ancient passage grave, dating to 3000 BC, reduced to just an overgrown, indiscernible mound now. There are more megalithic monuments on the northern confines of Saggart Hill, near the Slade Valley Golf Club, at Knockananiller and Knockandinny. Another passage tomb can also be found in Lugg Wood away to the north-east.

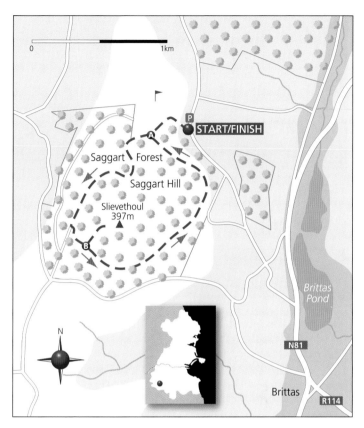

Route Description

Take the broad, surfaced track by the information board past two metal forest barriers. The track climbs gradually uphill and is flanked by mature conifers. Some of the area has also been replanted with larch and Sitka spruce.

Ignore a junction (Point A on the map) on the left and continue ahead. The Slade Valley golf course runs behind the trees and a metal gate away to your right.

The track straightens out after two switchbacks. A clearing on the right soon appears, giving fine vistas of fertile fields, farmland and the vast Kildare plains below.

Green and Orange Trail markers on Saggart Hill.

159

Masts on the highest point of Saggart Hill.

When the track forks, follow the Green/Orange Trail markers and turn left uphill. Masts can now be seen on a rise away to the left. Leave the trail when it forks again (Point B) and veer left towards the masts and reach the highest point on Saggart Hill.

The view from here is somewhat restricted by trees and the masts, and not as good as at the clearing earlier. When ready, retrace steps back to Point B then turn left to follow the Green/Orange Trail signs once again.

Soon, views across to the Kilbride hills of Seahan and Seefingan can be seen in the distance ahead beyond Saggart Forest.

As the track veers north-east, the Kilbride hills now rise away to your right. Views come and go through gaps in the deciduous woodland.

The track is soon flanked by conifers and descends to pass a broad lay-by on either side. Soon after you pass the lay-bys, another clearing appears on the right giving views down to Brittas Pond and some houses, with the Kilbride hills as the backdrop.

Soon after, the track is flanked by gorse bushes, whose coconut-scented flowers bloom bright yellow over the summer months.

Follow the track up a rise before it levels off to arrive back at the junction at Point A with the golf course ahead.

Turn right there and retrace steps back to the start.

The view from a clearing on the forest track at the eastern end of Saggart Hill towards Brittas Ponds, with the Kilbride hills in the distance.